LALIQUE

SHIRE PUBLICATIONS

LALIQUE

ERIC KNOWLES

SHIRE PUBLICATIONS

Published in Great Britain in 2012 by Shire Publications Ltd, Midland House, West Way, Botley, Oxford OX2 0PH, United Kingdom.

44-02 23rd Street, Suite 219, Long Island City, NY 11101, USA.

E-mail: shire@shirebooks.co.uk   www.shirebooks.co.uk

© 2011 Eric Knowles. First printed 2011. Reprinted 2012.

A CIP catalogue record for this book is available from the British Library.

Shire Collections no. 7   ISBN-13: 978 0 74780 828 2

Eric Knowles has asserted his right under the Copyright, Designs and Patents Act, 1988, to be identified as the author of this book.

Designed by Ken Vail Graphic Design, Cambridge, UK and typeset in Bembo.

Printed in China through Worldprint Ltd.

12 13 14 15 16   11 10 9 8 7 6 5 4 3 2

COVER IMAGE
Suzanne. A 1925 opalescent figurine designed to be fitted onto a bronze stand for illumination. Height 23 cm.

PAGE 2 IMAGE
A gold and *plique a jour* enamel pendant and chain fashioned as four damselflies contesting a central blue stone cabochon, created *c.* 1905. Width 7 cm. (Courtesy of Woolley & Wallis, Salisbury.)

DEDICATION
For my Parents

'A small thank you for providing me with the compass for my journey through life'

ACKNOWLEDGEMENTS
I would like to take this opportunity of thanking the following for their kind assistance not only for their much-valued advice but also for sharing their passion over many years for the all things Lalique:

Mr Silvio Denz and his colleagues at Lalique in London, Paris and Wingen; Jill Wark of Lewis Wark for whom nothing was ever too much trouble; Nicholas Dawes and Mark Waller for their constant friendship, inspiration and providing benchmark research and vital criticism after reading my manuscript; Glenn and Mary-Lou Utt for their infectious enthusiasm and giving me such memorable hospitality at their home in Wisconsin in years long gone by; Mr David Weinstein for his indomitable pioneering spirit and advice, as well as endless coffee on visits to his home in New York where I would gaze open-mouthed at his fabulous collection; Mr Robert Brooks, Chairman of Bonhams for allowing me access to the company's wonderful image archive; Mark Oliver and Will Gilding, my former colleagues at Bonhams in New Bond Street, London for their readiness to help provide images at the drop of a hat. The same holds true of another former colleague, Joy McCall, and long-time friend Fiona Baker, both of Christies, London and all at a time when they had far better things to do. To Michael Jeffrey of Woolley and Wallis, Salisbury for images and welcome advice from a much-respected authority; My son, Oliver Knowles for providing me with splendid images of Lalique's house in Paris and his much-appreciated support at all times; Andrew Stewart of Saffron Walden, photographer extraordinaire, who across three decades has set the exacting standards for showing Lalique glass at its best; Mirek Malevski for his support and ready access to his encyclopaedic knowledge of all things Lalique for which I am grateful and forever in awe; Raul Arantes and Mike Fenton for their advice over many years and their unstinting devotion both to the sale and purchase of great examples at their office in London's City Road; Christopher Vane Percy whose book *The Glass of Lalique – A Collectors Guide,* published in 1977, has always been recognised as the seminal work to appear in the English language and as such remains an important addition to my library; Madame Giselle Le Goff and colleagues at Nina Ricci, Paris, for kind permission to use an image of their famous *L'Air du Temps* perfume bottle. And finally to Nick Wright and Russell Butcher of Shire Books for their much-valued support and advice in making the book you are now holding actually exist.

Eric Knowles F.R.S.A.

CONTENTS

AUTHOR'S PREFACE

RENÉ LALIQUE was a rare individual: he possessed the ability to pursue and excel in two distinct careers, initially as an exclusive jewellery designer and later as the creator of stunning commercial glassware. His imaginative designs can both excite and occasionally shock, while his sheer versatility ensured his international commercial success through often uncertain times. In this book, I hope to show that – whatever the discipline or decade – Lalique's was a singular talent, which sought and achieved perfection in all creative endeavours.

Some readers may know me from BBC Television's *Antiques Roadshow*, on which I make regular appearances. When I'm recording one of these programmes – be it in Bournemouth or Barnsley – likely as not someone will bring me a piece of beautiful Lalique glassware. Or at least they will if I'm lucky.

I first encountered Lalique in the early 1970s, when I was working for an antique dealer in my native Lancashire. I came across a set of six dessert bowls moulded as scallop shells, each engraved 'R. Lalique, France'. I was intrigued and mesmerised by their curious milky blue opalescence, which my employer assured me was achieved by using a secret technique that Lalique had taken to his grave. This, I later discovered, was pure fantasy: Jobling and several French glassmakers had also made use of opalescence in their creations during the inter-war period. Nevertheless, the myth lent Lalique a certain mystique; I resolved to find out more.

In 1976, I moved down to London to join the Ceramics and Glass department of Bonhams auction house. The capital was awash with Lalique glass, the likes of which showed their creator to be far more inventive than the *Coquilles* bowls I had encountered Up North. Suddenly, I was introduced to inventive forms and exciting, yet subtle, moulded detail that had me further spellbound.

Lalique glassware is, of course, highly collectable. By the time I had graduated from being a lowly porter to overseeing and running the Decorative Arts department at Bonhams in 1981, the market was hungry for it. Remaining strong throughout the 1980s, Lalique prices plummeted with the recession of the early 1990s, but have now stabilised once more.

As with all antiques and collectables, it pays to arm yourself with reliable reference books and although I'm delighted that you're reading this one, I must stress that this is a gentle introduction to a subject that might eventually have you considering spending several hundred pounds for the definitive, but currently out of print, *Catalogue Raissone* (listed in the Bibliography). I do, however, recommend that you seek out a copy of the reprint of the 1932 Lalique trade catalogue, which is crammed with photographs and the official dimensions of each piece. These can often help to determine if a piece has been reduced in size by later repairs. Be warned: the Lalique glass market has many 'doctored' offerings, so it's as well to buy from a reputable dealer or a serious auction house. If the price tag appears to be cheap, ask yourself why.

Four decades on from my first 'close encounter', I am still in awe of the sheer fertility of this man's imagination. In my opinion, Lalique is unquestionably the premier glass designer of the twentieth century.

Opposite:
Detail of one of the frosted-glass angel panels on the doors of St Matthew's church at Millbrook, Jersey.

INTRODUCTION

RENÉ JULES LALIQUE entered this world in 1860 and, although born in the rural Champagne region, his family eventually set up home in Paris, where his father worked as a purveyor of fancy goods. The young René soon showed a talent for drawing, which was nurtured by return visits to his former pastoral playground. He found much to inspire him. Indeed, his keen observation of nature was to prove extremely important in later life, when he became apprenticed to the leading Parisian jeweller Louis Aucoc in 1876.

Lalique worked with Aucoc for two years, during which time he attended evening classes at the École des Arts Décoratifs. In 1878, he moved to London, where he enrolled at the Sydenham School of Art, which was reputedly housed in the Crystal Palace building that had originally been erected in Hyde Park for the 1851 Great Exhibition. Lalique was not the only notable French artist who gravitated to this part of south London, as the celebrated impressionists Édouard Manet and Claude Monet also found their way to the capital around this time. Many on the Continent and in the United States were starting to recognise Britain as a centre for new and radical artistic ideas, such as those initially championed by the Pre-Raphaelite Brotherhood of artists and writers, and further stimulated by the critiques and social writings of John Ruskin and William Morris. Their influence became evident in the exciting creations that emanated from the newly established craft guilds that had sprung up across the entire country.

Lalique returned to France in 1880 and is known to have worked as a freelance jewellery designer, supplying Aucoc (and others – including Cartier) with ideas that went into production, but for which he received no visible credit. Perhaps because of this, he made the decision in 1885 to purchase his own workshop from the jeweller Jules Destape. Within five years, his breathtaking jewellery was adorning the royalty and the well-to-do of both the Old and New worlds.

In 1886, Lalique married his first wife, Marie-Louise Lambert, with whom he had a daughter, Georgette, who died young in 1910. However, the marriage itself appears to have failed as by 1890 he had formed a new relationship with Augustine-Alice Ledru, daughter of the celebrated sculptor Auguste Ledru. Lalique eventually married Mlle Ledru on 8 July 1902, after the births of their daughter Suzanne (1892) and son Marc (1900).

Lalique had always been fascinated by glass production. During the early 1890s, he owned his own glass furnace, situated on the family estate at Clairefontaine, which he used for making the small glass items that he incorporated into his jewelled creations. By 1905, however, his interest in jewellery design had begun to wane, and his fascination with glass had started to grow. In 1907, he was approached by his neighbour, the celebrated perfumer François Coty, to design the embossed gilt paper labels for his scent bottles. Legend has it that Lalique took umbrage at the suggestion and undertook the commission on the strict understanding that he could design the bottles as well.

Opposite:
Chrysis. A satin-frosted figural car mascot designed in 1931. Height 14.5 cm.

After the introduction of Lalique's new vessels, Coty saw a truly dramatic increase in sales, which resulted in many prestigious French perfume houses knocking on the door of Lalique's new Place Vendôme showrooms to commission his talents for their own products. In 1907, Lalique leased his own commercial works at Combs-la-Ville, about 30 kilometres south-east of Paris. Here, he began to produce a demi-crystal type of glass that contained only half the usual lead oxide content. The result was a more malleable medium, which showed good definition alongside a warmer hue or colour. Demi-crystal continued as the preferred choice until as late as 1950, after which the company decided to favour the much whiter full lead crystal still used today.

This was to prove a pivotal period, and by 1911 glass dominated Lalique's new showrooms in the Place Vendôme. Ten years later, he set up the present-day glassworks in the rural village of Wingen-sur-Moder, located in the Alsace, near Strasbourg. Certainly by 1925, Lalique had become recognised as the country's leading commercial glassmaker and designer, with an ever-expanding repertoire that included not only perfume bottles, but also a huge variety of useful and decorative moulded glassware. Glancing through any catalogue from those inter-war years reveals a desirable and extensive selection that includes tableware, lighting, figures, car mascots, bowls, vases,

René Lalique in his studio, c. 1912. Note the Paon *table lamp on the desk.*

toilet boxes, clocks and much more. His choice of design often echoed his childhood fascination with nature, while his lean and sinuous ladies suggest a more mature appreciation and understanding of the female form. Lalique's women soon become instantly recognisable to the trained eye, whether they are cavorting nude in a Bacchanalian orgy, or adorned in gossamer drapery that might do little to hide their fine contours.

The Lalique company survived and prospered throughout the 1920s and '30s. Towards the end of this period, it was largely supported by an international nouveau riche clientele, which was able to weather the financial storm that blew in with the Wall Street Crash of 1929. Such buyers were keen to be seen as stylish and (above all) modern; they chose to project this image by adorning their dining rooms with Lalique's decidedly thin tableware or illuminating their interiors with his inventive light fittings, while fitting one of his twenty-nine car mascot designs onto their equally upmarket motor vehicles.

François Coty, the famous perfumer, c. 1910. Coty and Lalique were to enjoy a mutually beneficial business partnership for many years.

A silver-and-glass oval centrepiece, created c. 1903–05 and signed 'Lalique' on the right-hand edge. The maiden is festooned with seaweed and raised upon a pedestal of lily pads, while the outer surround includes four water nymphs, each grasping a dolphin from whose open jaws pour torrents of water in frosted glass. Height 59 cm. (Courtesy of the Gulbenkian Museum, Lisbon.)

The interior of No. 40 Cours la Reine (now Cours Albert Premier), c. 1902. (Courtesy of Lalique.)

René Lalique and his second wife Augustine-Alice, c. 1903.

Serpents. *This early bronze cheval mirror, created 1899–1900, is supported by a pair of patinated snakes. It once featured in Lalique's atelier and showrooms at No. 40 Cours la Reine (now Cours Albert Premier) in Paris. Height 169 cm. (Courtesy of the Gulbenkian Museum, Lisbon.)*

The pricing policy of this period purposely excluded the masses, in order to maintain the perceived exclusivity that was the mainstay of all French luxury goods. Despite his ability to produce on a large scale, Lalique was thus careful to limit his output. Although production records are no longer available, the manufacture of some of his designs can be measured in the hundreds and low thousands. Even so, profits continued to be high.

The design of this walnut gallery chair is attributed to René Lalique and Charles Lambert. Note the embossed leather back and gilt monogram.

In 1925, the Éxposition des Arts Décoratifs et Industriels Modernes – the famous Paris Exhibition – opened to the public. It is believed to be the origin of the term 'Art Deco'. Lalique was to play an important role in this opulent showcase, being commissioned to create the lighting for some of the most important salon interiors. However, his most recognisable contribution was the exhibition's foremost attraction: an enormous illuminated fountain. Rising to some 50 metres, this elegant structure comprised seventeen graduated tiers of octagonal sections, each supporting eight frosted and polished glass figurines of slender form and almost Madonna-like appearance. It was known as the *Source de la Fontaine*.

René Lalique's interest in the architectural possibilities of glass had begun at the start of the twentieth century, with the massive glass-and-steel doors he designed for his new home and atelier at No. 40 Cours la Reine (today known as Cours Albert Premier). The list of Lalique's later commissions includes decorative figural glass panels set into the luxurious interiors of the rail carriages of the Compagnie Internationale des Wagons-Lit, which took elegant, affluent passengers between Paris and the Côte d'Azur. However, perhaps his most adventurous designs were to be found in the SS *Normandie*, which was launched in 1932 and made its maiden voyage to New York in 1935. Described as a floating temple of Art Deco, the *Normandie* boasted the finest in French contemporary design. Lalique's

The distinctive Art Deco pavilion of Galeries Lafayette at the 1925 Éxposition des Arts Décoratifs et Industriels Modernes. (Bibliotheque des Arts Decoratifs, Paris, France/Archives Charmet/The Bridgeman Art Library.)

contribution took the form of the first-class dining room, which measured a staggering 91 metres and included an illuminated glass ceiling and side panels (with a dozen glass fountains thrown in for good measure). Alas, this remarkable vessel was destroyed by fire while at anchor in New York City harbour in 1942; but another of Lalique's architectural commissions still stands as testament to his genius.

Though often referred to as the 'Glass Church', St Matthew's at Millbrook on the Channel Island of Jersey looks anything but from the exterior. Only when entering this modernistic building is the visitor confronted by its massive glass cruciform, moulded with lily flowers above the altar with side screens and a Lady Chapel guarded by attendant angels.

René Lalique died in 1945 at the age of 85, being buried in the Père Lachaise Cemetry, Paris. However, the company – and the Lalique name – lived on, for René's son Marc took over the running of the firm, which by now had around 600 employees. While the majority of collectors are primarily interested in René Lalique-designed glassware produced during his lifetime, Marc had already shown his worth by skilfully marketing his father's work and was soon recognised as a highly competent designer and modeller in his own right.

During the years immediately after the Second World War, more and more of Marc's work began to grace the company catalogues, many of his sophisticated offerings showing a great synergy with the contemporary interiors of that time. Enthusiasts have been relatively slow to add his work to their cabinets and consequently his creations are, in the opinion of this writer, still relatively underpriced and well worth consideration. One example is his *Ange* (or Angel of Reims) wineglass, on which the angel's engraved and frosted wings partially envelope the bowl in a form that can only be described as pure sculpture (see page 116).

After Marc's death in 1977, his own daughter, Marie-Claude Lalique, became the company's Art Director, although she resisted the opportunity to become Chief Administrator like her father and grandfather. Marie-Claude was quick to establish her own personal and innovative approach and continued to do so until her untimely death in 2003. Her work not only shows maturity, but also an intelligent understanding of colour and its integration with daring sculptural forms. As with her father, her work has yet to make any significant impact on the secondary market, if only because the original owners are still enjoying her creations.

Today, the company continues its pursuit of distinctive design from its glassworks in Wingen-sur-Moder under the guidance of its new owner, Silvio Denz, himself a passionate collector of Lalique.

St Matthews church entrance doors inset with frosted glass angel panels in high relief.

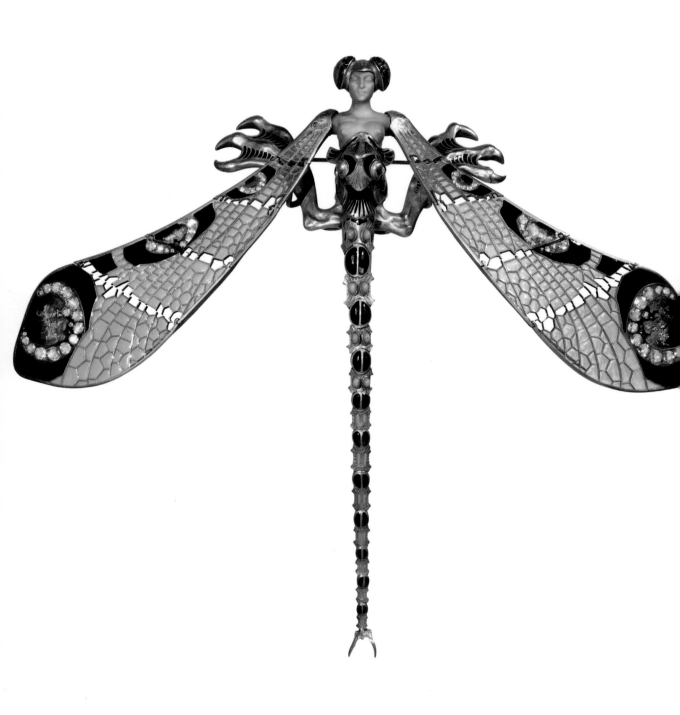

Chapter One

JEWELLERY

RENÉ LALIQUE'S childhood talent and passion for drawing, together with his keen observation of the natural world, was to propel him to the position of France's premier jeweller. The influence of boyhood days spent in the countryside of his mother's native Champagne first manifested itself in the small ivory panels that he would paint and later sell for pocket money. Although this interest appears to have been nurtured by his family, there is no record of any other relative sharing a similar gift.

Lalique moved to Paris while still an infant and had gained a scholarship to the Lycée Turgot by the age of twelve. Sadly, his father died when he was sixteen, making it imperative for the young René to find employment. By a stroke of good fortune, and his mother's rumoured tenacity, he managed to secure himself an apprenticeship with the foremost Parisian jeweller, Louis Aucoc.

Lalique worked with Aucoc for two years, after which time he went to London to study at the Sydenham School of Art. However, he returned to Paris in 1880 and took up employment with various other jewellery makers, including the firm of Auguste Petit fils. He was also credited with producing textile and wallpaper designs for a relative called Vuileret. Two years later, he decided to attend classes to study sculpture and etching techniques, making the all-important decision to set himself up as a freelance designer, supplying well-established outlets such as Jules Destape, Gariod, Jacta, Hamelin and his former employer Louis Aucoc. His growing design portfolio included both his more innovative creations and the more traditional gem-encrusted jewellery popularised by the established jewellery houses of Boucheron and Cartier.

In 1884, Lalique formed a two-year partnership with his friend Monsieur Varenne, who became responsible for selling his designs to various jewellery makers. 'Lalique et Varenne' worked from No. 84 Rue de Vaugirard in Paris. This was also the year that Lalique's designs were exhibited alongside the French Crown Jewels at the Exposition Nationale des Arts Industriels, held in the Louvre. It was here that his ideas caught the attention of one of the country's foremost jewellers, Alphonse Fouquet, who complimented Lalique thus: 'I am not aware of the existence of any contemporary jewellery designers and at last, here is one'. The following year, Lalique purchased the Place Gaillon workshop from his client, Jules Destape, who intended to retire to Algeria. It was here that Lalique devoted himself to jewellery production, in the company of his assistant, Paul Briançon, who was to remain his collaborator for the next twenty years.

Two years later he moved to Rue de Quatre Septembre and then in 1890 to larger premises at No. 20 Rue Thérèse, where he started to work with enamelled decoration, successfully selling a swallow design to Boucheron. His fascination with enamel developed and his jewels began to incorporate the *plique a jour* technique,

Opposite:
Femme Libellule.
A gold-and-enamelled corsage ornament, created c. 1897–8. The articulated dragonfly has wings of plique a jour *enamel inset with diamonds. Its slender thorax features multiple chalcedony and chrysoprase graduated cabochons. The upper torso is carved in chrysoprase. Height 23 cm. (Courtesy of the Gulbenkian Museum, Lisbon.)*

Opposite top:
Swallow. *An early and transitional jewel in gold and enamel, inset with diamonds, created by Lalique in collaboration with Paul Briançon in 1887. The jewel is fashioned in platinum and gold, with coloured champlevé enamel, rose and brilliant cut diamonds. The eyes are cabochon rubies. Height 10.6 cm. (Private Collection.)*

Opposite bottom:
A gold, enamel and opal wooded landscape plaque inset with diamonds, created c. 1898–9. This jewel illustrates Lalique's ability to capture the natural world in precious materials and invoke a beautiful dreamlike vision. Height 5 cm. (Courtesy of the Gulbenkian Museum, Lisbon.)

Left:
The celebrated French actress Sarah Bernhardt, c. 1895. Lalique met her in 1891 and went on to design several jewels for her.

whereby opaque and semi-translucent enamels are secured in an open filigree design, rather like a stained-glass window.

Lalique continued to supply designs to the leading jewellers of the time and some of his early creations – featured at the 1889 Paris Exposition Universelle – were credited both to Boucheron and Vever. It is interesting to consider that both these famous makers were primarily concerned with *joaillerie*, where the emphasis was on the use of single-colour stones. Lalique's attention, however, was rapidly becoming more concerned with the art of *bijouterie*, where the designer placed more importance on artistic form and was willing to embrace asymmetry and the use of multi-coloured stones and non-precious materials.

In 1895, Lalique exhibited his own jewellery (as opposed to his designs made by other people) under his own name at the Salon de la Société des Artistes Français. From here, his work began to demonstrate strong sculptural elements, occasionally borrowing from classicism, while showing a willingness to introduce the exaggerated and sinuous curves of the prevailing Art Nouveau style. Throughout the decade, his goldwork showed a similar tendency, using interlaced branches or whiplash scrollwork that provide the perfect setting for his sculptural fantasies.

During these years, Lalique's extensive imagination was unleashed in designs that clarified his acute perception and empathy with the dynamics that govern the organic world. The jewels started to betray a willingness to capture specific moments in time, whether relating to growth, decay or rebirth. Indeed, it was this unique talent to convey a sense of both mood and atmosphere that set him apart from his contemporaries (although many would try to copy him).

In 1896, he created a horn-and-ivory bracelet that featured a winter landscape of engraved and moulded glass. This showed him not to be averse to incorporating relatively modest materials alongside precious and semi-precious gemstones like onyx, coral, jasper and opal. When considering an object like this bracelet, it becomes apparent that its intrinsic value is completely overshadowed by the artistry of the design and the craftsmanship demanded in its making. Having recognised the possibilities offered by horn, which when heated becomes a surprisingly malleable material, he set about designing a series of breathtaking hair combs. Lalique explored the sculptural potential of horn further by embellishing it with precious stones and by employing carving, pressing and staining techniques to elevate its status.

A gold-and-enamel corsage ornament, created 1898–1900, fashioned as a bow with a central white peacock flanked by a curvilinear network of tail feathers inset with diamonds and opal cabochon 'eyes'. The peacock enjoyed great popularity with continental Art Nouveau designers and British and American exponents of the Arts and Crafts movements. Height 9.3 cm. (Courtesy of the Gulbenkian Museum, Lisbon.)

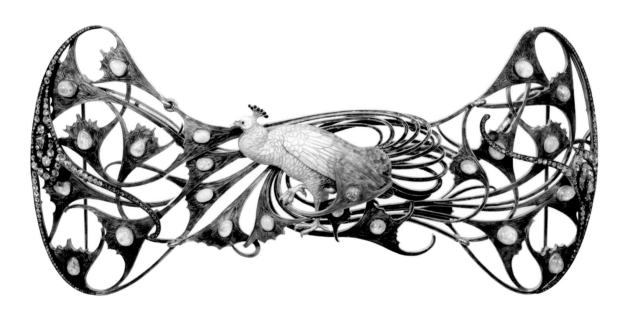

A horn-and-tinplate necklace, fashioned as opposing symmetrical grasshopper panels. The insects support baroque pearls in their upper and lower claws. Lalique is known to have favoured the use of thinly walled buffalo horn imported from South America and India. This piece was created c. 1902–03; grasshoppers also feature in Lalique's later glass designs. Diameter 19.5 cm. (Courtesy of the Gulbenkian Museum, Lisbon.)

His creativity soon became manifest in all manner of wonderful pieces inspired by nature. His boyhood passion for flowers, fruit, fish, insects and reptiles were all cast into his repertoire to take either centre stage or play supporting roles.

Throughout his life, this creative talent was regularly supported by a readiness to experiment, several of his jewels incorporating delicate ivory-and-metal plaques produced using the *tour à réduire* technique. Although the technology for scaling down complex detail by transferring from a large-scale original had already been used by medallists and coin designers, Lalique is thought to have been the first to adopt the method for jewellery design (although he was by no means the last). Perhaps the most dramatic results may be found in the art of enamelling and in particular the technique known as *plique a jour*, whereby both opaque and translucent

A horn, gold and enamel hair comb, created c. 1901–02. This 'drone and umbels' piece suggests Japanese inspiration in its observational yet relatively unconventional composition. The umbel flowers, carved in horn, provide a ready platform for six gold colour-enamelled worker bees. Height 16 cm. (Courtesy of the Gulbenkian Museum, Lisbon.)

enamels are suspended within an elaborate network of cells. The method follows closely that of Chinese *cloisonné* enamels, in which metal wires are applied to a metal base to form a design into which coloured paste enamels are placed. These are subsequently heated in a small kiln, resulting in the enamels fusing to the metal base. The *plique a jour* technique differs only by laying the metal wires and intended design onto a thin metal base. This burns away during the firing, leaving behind a magical effect that resembles stained glass.

Right: An oxidised silver and opalescent glass pendant, hung with a baroque pearl, created 1898–1900. The moulded mask is set within a silver surround of flowing tresses, adorned with poppies. Lalique's use of baroque or blister pearls began around 1897, having previously been favoured by Renaissance jewellers. Height of pendant 9.6 cm. (Courtesy of the Gulbenkian Museum, Lisbon.)

Below: A gold-framed brooch created in or before 1902, inset with diamonds and featuring the central carved ivory figure of an angel in prayer, with tall enamelled wings, flanked by jade cabochons of spinach green. Signed Lalique on the top left edge. Height 5.2 cm. (Courtesy of the Gulbenkian Museum, Lisbon.)

*Above: A gold, enamel
and glass bracelet, signed
on the fastener, created
c. 1900–01. This jewel
confirms Lalique's interest
in incorporating semi-
translucent glass images
within more precious
materials. Here, he places
moulded-glass owls upon
pine branches against a
sky of azure blue enamel.
Height 6.1 cm. (Courtesy
of the Gulbenkian
Museum, Lisbon.)*

*Centre: A gold-and-
enamel 'plaque de cou'
or dog collar, with pine-
cone and branch design,
c. 1900. Width 10.5 cm.*

*Below: A gold, silver and glass corsage ornament, created c. 1903–04 as two opposing scarab beetles in black enamelled silver contesting
a central facet-cut and polished tourmaline. Height 5.2 cm.*

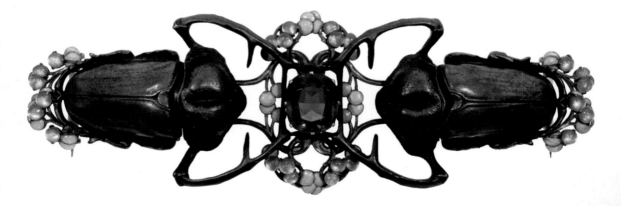

Serpents. *A gold-and-enamel corsage jewel, created 1898–9 and modelled as eight open-jawed snakes entwined by and pendant from a single sentinel snake. Signed Lalique on the upper right edge. Height 21 cm.*

Lalique devotee Calouste Gulbenkian, c. 1895. Gulbenkian earned the nickname 'Mr 5 per cent', a reference to his supposed holdings in the emerging petro-chemicals industry. His highly important collection of Lalique is on permanent display in the Gulbenkian Museum, Lisbon.

Lalique was fortunate to be able to call upon the services of master enameller Eugene Feuilatre, who in later years would achieve international fame as France's greatest exponent of this type of enamel artistry. Several of Feuilatre's masterworks are on display in the Musée d'Orsay in Paris. The ultimate expression of *plique a jour* is undeniably Lalique's imposing *Femme Libellule* corsage, purchased by Calouste Gulbenkian and considered by many to be the centrepiece of the highly important collection he would eventually bequest to the Gulbenkian Museum in Lisbon, Portugal.

Well before the advent of the twentieth century, Lalique had developed a fascination with glassmaking and had already experimented with it, incorporating both clear and opalescent glass in his jewels and precious objets d'art. Such experimentation would often focus upon surface decoration. This is shown to good effect on the *Poppy Maiden* pendant (see page 25), whose semi-opaque facial expression is covered with an opalescent enamel surface. The more usual opaque glass was of a type known as *pâte de verre*, which is created when coloured glass paste is pressed into a heat-resistant mould and then heated to a temperature that causes the material to fuse. The technique had been known since antiquity, but had recently been revived – to much acclaim – by Lalique's fellow countryman, Henri Cros. In later years, the Daum brothers further developed its potential at their glassworks in Nancy, as did their former employee Amalric Walter and Gabriel Argy-Rousseau.

An important stimulus for both applied and decorative arts in Paris and Britain came in the guise of Siegfried Bing, a German orientalist and entrepreneur, who established the soon-to-be-influential journal *Le Japon* in 1888 and owned a gallery, La Maison de l'Art Nouveau, from which the term 'Art Nouveau' is said to have been derived. The gallery sold all manner of important decorative arts, including the work of Emile Gallé, Georges de Feure, Hector Guimard (designer of the now iconic Metro entrances for the Paris Exposition of 1900) and Louis Comfort Tiffany.

Above left:
A gold-and-enamelled brooch in the form of a Cicada, the wings in plique a jour *enamel, terminated with diamonds, designed c. 1902. The body is mottled green glass, with diamond eyes in gold collets. Length 5.1 cm. (Courtesy of Wartski, London.)*

Above:
The Kiss. *A gold, enamel and ivory brooch, created 1900–2. Lalique encloses his two lovers within a frame of dense gold and lapis blue enamelled foliage. Although the carved-ivory characters are mostly hidden, the jewel loses nothing in the strength of its sensuality. Height: 7.2 cm. (Courtesy of the Gulbenkian Museum, Lisbon.)*

A gold brooch applied with mother of pearl, designed c. 1900, engraved with two cockerels contesting a central pearl, the reverse of the brooch identically engraved on its gold back. Width 6 cm. (Courtesy of Wartski, London)

Lalique was quick to recognise the value of associating with what was rapidly becoming the most important venue (and shop window) for the best in contemporary design. He duly consigned several of his jewels for display. The appreciation both he and Bing shared for Japanese art was an important factor in Lalique's decision to show at the gallery. Its influence cannot be overstated when considering that the Japanese approach to isolating and observing nature was unmistakable in many of his own pieces. However, it was his offering at the Paris Exposition Universelle of 1900 that confirmed his reputation as being the most admired and sought after jeweller of his generation. By now, Lalique numbered several crowned heads of Europe among his clientele, who would soon include the British Queen Alexandra, alongside numerous members of the aristocracy, heads of state and the wealthy families of the New World.

Lalique's dramatic display the Paris Exposition Universelle of 1900, before a composite bronze grille of sensually sculpted winged maidens.

Lalique's window display incorporated a decorative grille that featured five patinated bronze winged maidens, draped with gossamer clear gauze. Above their heads, he created a nocturnal sky in grey gauze, inhabited by black velvet bats and sprinkled with isolated stars. This was the pure theatre that formed a backdrop for his sensational selection of jewels and works of art. It attracted endless crowds of onlookers keen to marvel at their exquisite craftsmanship. The scenario was captured by the artist Félix Vallotton in his woodblock print, *Lalique's Window Display.*

The advent of the new century witnessed the introduction of jewellery that sought to emulate Lalique's creations. As a result, the market became flooded with debased jewels of questionable merit. Lalique's response was to forsake jewellery design in favour of glassmaking, although his interest in jewellery design and manufacture would soon be reawakened. However, his chosen medium for all later jewellery creations was to pave the way for a much larger potential market, while fitting neatly into his new career as a commercial glass designer.

The earliest examples made in about 1910 at his Combs-la-Ville works were of relatively simple design. They were either circular or bar brooches, with moulded decorative detail reflected through a silvered or coloured foil back, all held within a gilt copper mount stamped 'Lalique' on the back plate. The subject matter might include cornflowers, grasshoppers, deer, birds, snakes or his classic semi-nude maidens. Similar themes were applied to his colourful translucent glass pendants produced in various shaped outlines designed to be suspended from colour-coordinated silk cords, hung with tassels. Other clear decorative glass pendants were intaglio moulded and frosted, and once again suspended from silk cords.

As usual, Lalique's choice of motif was carefully adapted to suit the basic design. One features a splendid coiled snake, succulent berries and an oval panel displaying several opposing wasps (the panel was supplied in blue or black glass). Another, much rarer pendant took the form of a blister pearl, enamelled in blue or black with a shoal of slender fish. Lalique also fashioned several perfume bottle pendants of small size, similarly suspended. A number of coloured beaded-glass elasticated bracelets and necklaces were also produced, for which each individual bead might be modelled

Félix Vallotton's woodblock of Lalique's window at the Paris Exposition Universelle of 1900.

An enamel and gem set plaque de cou *in the form of a stylised pansy flower, decorated with opaque cream* plique a jour *enamel. The centre of the bloom is finished with foil-backed deep-blue enamel. The flower is highlighted by graduations of pavé set diamonds radiating from the centre into the petals. Signed Lalique on the lower edge. Width 5.5 cm.*

A gold-and-enamelled pendant modelled as a pair of large and smaller damselflies encircling a single opal of near-triangular form. Signed Lalique. Height 9.5 cm.

as a barrel, berry or an individual flower head such as lily of the valley. Some necklaces were moulded with decorative designs that spanned several panel beads. These *colliers* were intended to be worn close to the neck.

Despite the modern emphasis on Lalique's glassware, his jewellery continues to enjoy a reputation for quality. Interest may have been tempered by the relative scarcity of complete examples as, by the very nature of the medium, all Lalique's jewellery was prone to accidental damage. One might suggest that any search would be well worth the time spent.

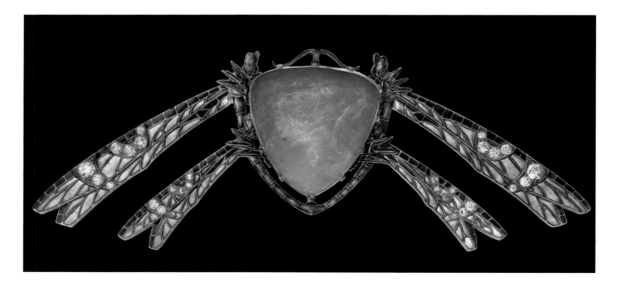

Figurine se Balançant.
*A glass pendant, designed
in 1919. Height 6 cm.*

Libellules. *An opalescent glass pendant with silk cord and tassels, designed in 1920. Height 4.2 cm.*

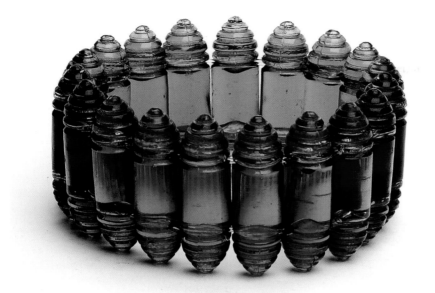

Creneaux. *An elasticated
bracelet in electric-blue
glass, designed in 1928.
Diameter 4.5 cm.*

Left to right: Colombes.
*An electric-blue frosted-
glass pendant featuring a
single maiden with flower-
bedecked hair and two
doves, designed 1920.
Height 4cm;* Graines.
*An electric-blue triangular
frosted-glass pendant
moulded with swirling
berry branches and pierced
to receive three pendant
blue-silk tassels, designed
1920. Height
5 cm;* Cabochon
Feuilles. *A small blue-
stained mounted and foil-
backed brooch, moulded
with overlapping tapering
leaves, designed 1920.
Diameter 3.3 cm.*

Chapter Two

PERFUME BOTTLES

RENÉ LALIQUE is known to have been designing and retailing decorative bottles, flasks and drinking glasses from his Place Vendôme premises as early as 1905. However, further impetus to concentrate his energy and talent entirely on glass has often been attributed to a meeting that took place with his neighbour two years later.

Born in Corsica and christened Francisco Giuseppe Spoturno, François Coty had established his Maison de Coty perfume shop at No. 23 Place Vendôme. He decided to approach Lalique and ask him to design the embossed gilt paper labels for his perfume bottles. Lalique is reputed to have insisted that he be given responsibility for the overall design of both bottles and labels; Coty, wisely as later events were to prove, agreed to his terms. Lalique's initial problem was that of production, having at that moment no commercial glassworks of his own. Consequently, the earliest bottles were made by Legras et Cie at its Saint-Denis factory in Paris. These early creations differ significantly from those eventually produced by Lalique at his Combs-la-Ville glassworks. From 1909, when production began, Lalique used a different proportion of lead oxide in the glass mix. Legras incorporated 24 per cent, thereby producing a full lead crystal, whereas Lalique eventually preferred to use 12 per cent to achieve a demi-crystal.

The collaboration between Lalique and Coty – two giants of the French luxury retail trade – proved a huge success, even though some of Lalique's initial designs were relatively simple, making use as they did of clear panel-form bottles, whose decorative elements were restricted to the moulded and frosted stoppers. It is important to note that most (though not all) Coty fragrances were packaged in Lalique glass bottles and that one design might be used for as many as a dozen essences. Coty also commissioned glass bottles from Baccarat, which were supplied with similar labels.

It is worth emphasising that, for generations, perfume was purchased in simple utilitarian flasks and then decanted into the customer's own perfume bottle fashioned in glass, porcelain or metal. The idea of purchasing perfume at an affordable price in a ready-made beautiful glass vessel, doing away with the fiddly business of pouring the liquid into it through a tiny funnel, was greeted with immediate approval.

Particularly rare nowadays are the rectangular polished-wood tester boxes that were supplied to accredited retailers for shop-counter display. Each of these elegant cases held twelve perfume bottles. Their hinged covers and interiors featured an embossed gilt metal plaque sporting three willowy nude maidens, each holding a small vessel from which cloud-like vapours emanated, spelling 'Les Parfums de Coty'. (Lalique's signature was visible in the bottom-right corner.)

The Combs-la-Ville factory was near Fontainebleau, some 55 kilometres south-east of Paris, in an area that boasted high-quality silica. Unsurprisingly, the region

Opposite
Quatre Cigales by 'Maison Lalique', designed in 1910 and featuring clear and frosted glass. Height 13 cm.

Above: L'Effleurt *for Coty, a bottle in clear, frosted and stained glass, designed in 1908. This is the second version of the* L'Effleurt *bottle, the first featuring a faceted ball stopper. The figural design was adapted for both paper and patinated brass labels and would appear on many other vessels. Height 11 cm.*

Above:
Petites Feuilles *by 'Maison Lalique', designed in 1910 and incorporating frosted and turquoise-stained glass. Height 10.2 cm.*

Right:
Embossed gilt metal plaque fitted to the interior lid of Coty tester boxes, signed 'R. Lalique', designed in 1912.

had been attracting glassmakers for several hundred years. In his essential book *Lalique Glass* (Crown, 1986), Nicholas Dawes suggested that 'Lalique probably employed between fifty and a hundred people initially at Combs-la-Ville chiefly in the manufacture of commercial perfume bottles. The technology for mass production was partly borrowed from the French wine and Pharmaceutical industries'. The principal methods of production were *presse soufflé*, where molten glass is blown by mouth or mechanical means into a twin-section hinged mould, and *aspire soufflé*, where the same glass is sucked into a mould, thereby creating a vacuum inside it. Lalique was never slow to embrace technological advances and decided to use long-lasting, hinged steel moulds, which – while initially expensive – delivered greater numbers of bottles and stoppers, and allowed for the crisp definition of fine detail.

Some of Lalique's earliest perfume bottles had their detail further enhanced by the use of coloured staining (*patine*) – a technique that would play an important role throughout his expanding catalogue of works. The stoppers were solid cast in half-section moulds before being ground with a textured surface. This acted as a watertight seal once inserted into a neck with a similarly ground inner surface. Both

A Coty burr-wood counter display and tester box, c. 1912.

Cyclamen for Coty, with original presentation box, designed in 1909. Height 13.5 cm.

stopper and bottle base were then hand engraved with matching control numbers, making later marriages and replacements easier to determine.

For Lalique, each stopper design was of paramount importance. He would eventually create sixteen individual examples for Coty, alongside promotional pieces, advertising signs and tester boxes. These early commissions, produced between 1909 and 1915, are considered to be some of the finest, and consequently the most desirable, of all Lalique's commercial perfume bottles. One of his earliest bottles for Coty, produced in 1907–10, was *L'Effleurt de Coty* (The Caress of Coty), which makes use of an upright rectangular panel enclosing a sinuous nymph emerging from a honeysuckle-type flower, all above the integral-moulded label. Lalique was to produce a second version, whereby the stopper was moulded as a stylised cicada. Both this and the figural panel were patinated in either a grey or sepia-brown stain, with the rest of the bottle polished clear.

If this bottle might be considered sensual and mystical in its play on the female form, Lalique's 1910 design for Coty's *Ambre Antique* is unquestionably classical and sober. Modelled as a slender, near-bullet form, with narrow neck and everted toprim, the bottle is depress (or intaglio) moulded with four classical maidens attired in floor-length robes, their hair gathered *en chignon* as they hold small sprigs of blossom. The 'Grecian'-type maidens and the stylised floral stopper are accentuated and delineated with sepia brown against an overall satin-frosted surface. Lalique's intaglio-moulded signature in bold capital letters is incorporated beneath the feet of one of the women.

In 1909, Lalique revisited his fascination with all things magical by offering a truly beautiful design for Coty's *Cyclamen* essence. Taking a slender tapering panel-form bottle, he intaglio moulded four lithe fairies below each shoulder, their elongated wings falling pendant towards the base. Each fairy is well defined using a green stain. The stopper took the form of a simple disc, moulded with 'Cyclamen, Coty, Paris'. Lalique was eventually to produce three slightly different versions, with the second featuring a plain stopper and the third being given a much narrower collar neck (but with the original stopper).

That same year saw the introduction of one of Lalique's earliest coloured-glass perfume bottles. Modelled as a stylised flower head, the squat circular vessel is incise moulded with the label 'Au Coeur des Calices'. The stopper is shaped in the form of a bumblebee. 'The Heart of the Calix' refers to that part of a flower head or plant from which perfumers are able to extract the essential oils needed in the blending of a complex essence. The bottle enjoyed an enduring popularity.

Cigalia. *A clear, frosted and green-stained bottle and stopper with original presentation box, designed in 1910 (height 12.6 cm). Cigalia was made in three sizes, including a miniature travelling version and a larger Eau de Toilette bottle. Lalique also designed a similar lotion bottle with tapered shoulders. (Courtesy of Christie's.)*

The bottle on the right is a 'Maison Lalique' piece called Meplat Deux Figurines, *designed in 1912 (height 12 cm). On the left is* Leurs Ames *for D'Orsay, designed in 1920 (height 12.5 cm).*

The collaboration between Lalique and Coty resulted in a dramatic increase in sales and a discussion of all Coty's further commissions is beyond the scope of this book. However, it should be noted that the success of the collaboration resulted in other prominent perfume houses approaching Lalique to commission similar bottles for their own ranges. As early as 1910, Lalique had designed a remarkable bottle in three sizes for Roger et Gallet's *Cigalia*, modelled as a clear-and-frosted upright panel-form bottle moulded on all four shoulders with a cicada beetle and a simple leaf-form stopper. The ensemble was sold in an embossed and shaped wooden presentation box, which featured a pair of cicada beetles heightened in silver wash and flanking the integral label, 'Cigalia, Roger et Gallet, Paris'.

From here on, the use of stylish 'Perfume Presentations' became fundamentally important to Lalique's marketing policy. In 1909, he also designed a bottle which utilised a stopper for its primary decorative element – a first for Lalique. *Paquerettes* makes use of a simple clear bottle of relatively squat and shouldered form and a clear-and-frosted stopper of crescent or 'tiara' shape, moulded with a regular spray of daisy flower heads on slender stems, all to stunning effect.

Art Nouveau maidens were incorporated into bottles as late as 1915. One example is *Flausa*, where the subject is modelled in low relief in a kneeling posture attired in a diaphanous robe. Roger et Gallet continued to commission bottles until 1922, when the taste for all things Oriental began to infiltrate western design once again.

Le Jade saw Lalique adopt not only a Chinese snuff bottle shape, but also the use of an opalescent jade green glass detailed with an exotic bird. The presentation box echoed

Below left:
Le Jade *for Roger et Gallet in opaque jade green, designed in 1926. Height 8 cm.*

Below right:
Elegance *for D'Orsay, designed in 1922. Height 9.8 cm.*

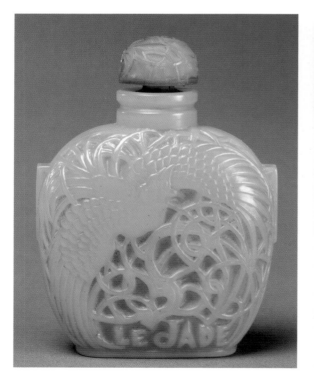

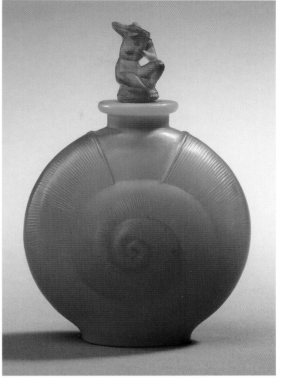

Above left:
Bouchon Mures.
A 'Maison Lalique'
clear-and-red enamelled
bottle with deep-red tiara
stopper moulded with
blackcurrants, designed
1920. Height 11 cm.

Above right:
Amphitrite *by 'Maison*
Lalique', in opaque
jade green glass, designed
c. 1920. Height 9.5 cm.

Left:
Vers le Jour *for Worth,*
featuring toned amber,
designed in 1926.
Height 7.5 cm.

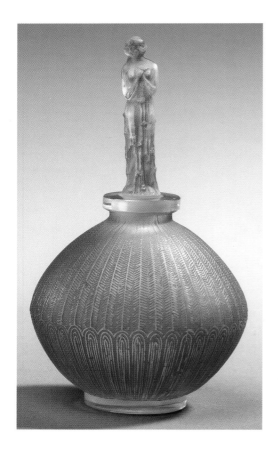

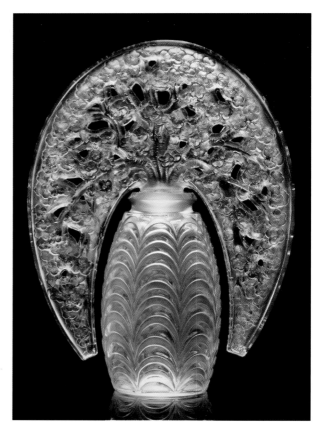

Above: Roses *for D'Orsay, designed in 1919. A plain 'Maison Lalique' version was also produced. Height 19 cm.*

Above right: Bouchon Fleurs de Pommier. *A 'Maison Lalique' bottle in clear with blue staining, designed 1919. Height 14 cm.*

the same oriental exoticsm; covered in black silk, the drop-over cover resembled a Japanese *inro* – a type of small sectional box often in lacquer and suspended from a waistband. Other pre-war commissions came from Arys, Rosine and D'Orsay. Introduced in 1913, the *Ambre D'Orsay* tapering panel-form bottle was produced in polished black glass. An uneasy sense of the macabre is suggested by the use of a shrouded figure at each corner, the mood being lifted by the incised floral motif on the top of the square-section stopper. The use of polished, jet-black glass was a combination Lalique repeated two years later with his *Mystère D'Orsay*. The introduction of this polished black glass (which never fails to add an air of elegance) appears to have been quite limited, although it was to find further use in vase, inkwell and jewellery designs.

Lalique had always recognised that the expanding market for perfume bottles need not be restricted to his perfume industry clientele. Consequently, he had introduced his own 'Maison Lalique' bottles as early as 1910. This range was sold empty, allowing purchasers to decant their own choice of perfume into each. We tend to accept the term 'Maison Lalique' as referring to those bottles that pre-date 1945, although at the time of writing there is no evidence to suggest any commercial glass output after the German occupation of the Alsace in 1939. The 1932 catalogue records seventy-eight individual designs, although nine further examples were added after the Second World War by Lalique's son Marc and granddaughter Marie-Claude.

Lalique's sculptural flair comes into play with several 'Maison' bottles, especially where the decorative and focal element is largely confined to the stopper. These tend to be relatively oversized and of horseshoe, crescent or tiara form and typically moulded with flowers or fruit. They were available in both frosted and coloured glass. In contrast, the actual bottles tend to be simpler, tapering towards the neck and occasionally striped in matching coloured enamel. Stoppers that are purely sculptural are rare and include *Amphitrite* (the wife of Poseidon), who is shown kneeling with a conch shell held to one ear. Measuring no more than 1.5 cm, a single frosted example of this stopper realised £800 at auction in the 1980s. Introduced in 1920, the bottle itself is modelled as a compressed coiled shell. It was produced in clear and frosted glass, as well as several (much rarer) coloured versions.

One of Lalique's earliest designs to incorporate a figural stopper is his *Meplat Deux Figurines*, introduced in 1912. This makes use of two reversed nude maidens with arms extended and hands holding their long Rapunzel-like hair. When inserted into its compressed rectangular bottle, which features two slender maidens holding branches of blossom within a central solid medallion, the overall effect is simply stunning. This goes some way to explain why, in Lalique's 1932 catalogue, most perfume bottles are priced in the region of 100 francs, whereas *Meplat Deux Figurines* costs significantly more, at 450 francs.

Above left:
Ambre D'Orsay. *A polished black-and-white stained bottle, designed 1911. Height 13 cm.*

Above right
Parfam 'A' *for Lucien Lelong, with black enamel and chrome presentation box, designed in 1929. Height of box 12 cm.*

45

With the advent of the 1930s, Lalique's 'Maison' bottles continued to use strong floral elements, compared to many of his corporate commissions, which began to embrace distinctly minimalist forms. This is well illustrated by shapes used in the promotion of several Worth essences, such as *Sans Adieu, Je Reviens* and *Imprudence* where each, often radical, form is devoid of any ornamentation. These were unquestionably forms that reflected the advance of the 'Moderne' into commercial design as dictated by a new machine age of concrete, steel and glass that was soon to be enveloped into the dark clouds of war in 1939.

Lalique was clearly a designer who could respond to the prevailing winds of artistic change, as well as determine their direction.

Left: Dans la Nuit *for Worth. A clear-glass bottle with cobalt-blue staining, designed in 1924. Height 14 cm.*

Opposite top left: Panier de Roses. *A 'Maison Lalique' frosted-glass bottle, designed in 1913. Height 10 cm.*

Opposite top middle: Danseuses Egyptiennes. *A vaporiser (atomiser) for Marcel et Bardel, designed in 1926. Height 15.5 cm.*

Opposite top right: Figurines. *A frosted and sienna-stained vaporiser or atomiser for Marcas et Bardel, designed in 1926. Height 9.3 cm.*

Opposite bottom: A clear-and-frosted counter display panel for Parfums D'Orsay.

Left: Althea *also known as* Narkiss *for Roger et Gallet, frosted and enamelled, designed 1912. It is shown alongside its original embossed-card presentation box. Height 10 cm.*

Chapter Three

VASES

L ALIQUE APPROACHED THE DESIGN of all utilitarian objects with the vision of a sculptor, leaving one in little doubt that, whatever his chosen subject, the outcome is unquestionably a work of art. For some, the idea of using any of his vases as a functional flower container is simply unthinkable. The full range of Lalique's vases offers a captivating insight into his ability to adapt his boundless imagination to create designs that appealed to clients across a period of time that witnessed massive changes both in society and in artistic taste.

Lalique's earliest vases belong to the closing decade of the nineteenth century. They employ moulded decoration that echoes the emerging Art Nouveau style, while nodding occasionally to classical subjects from ancient Greece and Rome. Approximately 200 vase designs are known to have been produced but, as with so much of his output, possibly half as many again never made it from the initial design stage and into production.

The manufacturing process involved the use of hinged twin-section steel moulds which, although initially expensive, allowed for detailed precision casting. As a result, mould lines are sometimes evident, although Lalique was often able to blend such telltale signs into the overall decoration. The actual production techniques employed necessitated blowing the molten glass into the moulds, using either the traditional hand-held blowpipe method or pneumatic air, depending on the size of the vessel. An alternative process saw the molten glass poured into a mould and then forced into the decorative detailing by means of a plunger. Once the desired piece is removed from the mould, it has to undergo a gradual cooling or annealing process, where the timing involved is a critical consideration – too soon and the glass is liable to fracture as a result of internal stresses. After this, the piece is ready for any secondary processing such as the removal of excess glass, acid frosting or surface patination and polishing.

The appeal and consequent desirability of any vase depends on several factors, including size, colour and manufacturing technique. Other important considerations are condition and rarity, with the latter sometimes difficult to determine, as no factory records appear to exist detailing output numbers prior to 1945. As determined collectors regularly vote with their wallets, the most desirable vases, as one might imagine, are invariably the most expensive. Vases moulded in strong translucent colours, alongside those moulded in a solid jet-black colour, are relatively rare. The jet-black examples were actually composed from an extremely dense purple, red or green colour that mimics a black appearance. Lalique introduced a wide spectrum of colours to his vases, which were sold at premium prices and which today are much sought after – especially those that are 'cased'.

Cased vases are made by blowing coloured glass into a mould, followed by a layer of opalescent glass gathered from a separate pot; sometimes another layer of the

Opposite
Aigrettes. *A satin-frosted vase, designed in 1926. This large and heavy piece was moulded with a complex yet delicate design of fanciful egrets defined by blue staining. Height 25.7 cm.*

Above left:
Monnaie du Pape. *An amethyst
and satin-frosted vase, designed in
1914. This is one of the earliest
Lalique vases to be produced in
several colours. Height 23 cm.*

Above right:
Formose. *A jade green cased vase,
designed in 1924: a popular piece
which was produced in several
colours. Height 18 cm.*

Left:
Sauterelles. *A clear, blue and
green-stained vase, designed in
1913. Multi-colour staining is rare
for Lalique glassware. Height 28 cm.*

Opposite:
Violettes. *An opalescent and satin-
frosted vase, designed in 1921.
A classic Lalique combination,
where inventive form and simple
moulded leaf-and-stem design result
in an unusual yet harmonious piece.
Height 16 cm.*

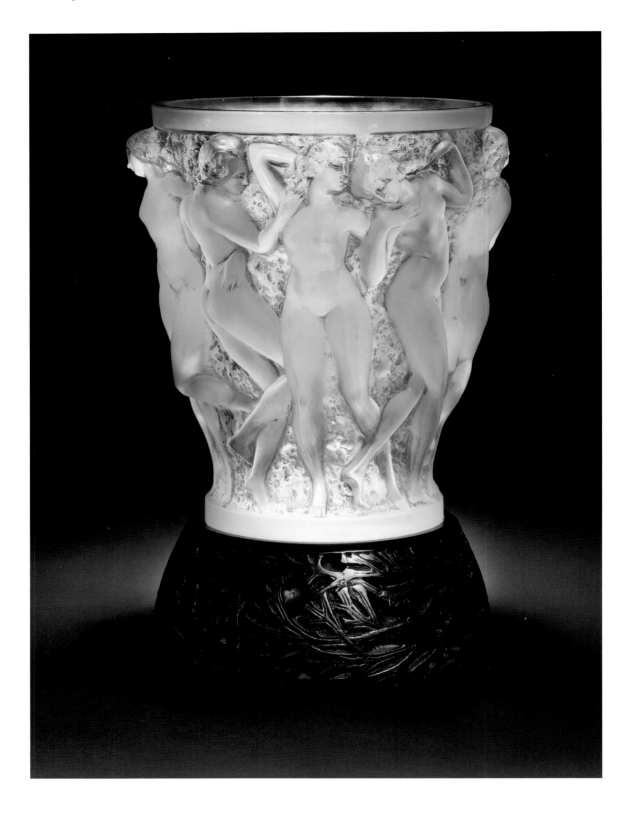

same coloured glass is added. The finished vase is usually heavier and exhibits an opaque appearance, with the 'sandwich' effect evident on the polished circular top rims. Whereas cased vases often attract high prices at auction, the simpler clear-and-frosted pieces tend to be far more affordable, although both rarity and size can sometimes elevate them.

The use of colour staining, or *patine* also helps to add desirability by accentuating the definition of the moulded detail. A word of caution is needed when examining colour staining, as some original Lalique vases (and other items) have been subject to later or additional staining. The recognition of later staining is largely dependent upon an understanding of the original colours used and one other significant fact: early staining is susceptible to wear if subjected to excessive washing and rubbing, whereas the modern coloured stain tends to be permanent. This is also applicable to the use and application of denser black enamel, which Lalique used to great effect on vases such as *Tourbillons*, *Oranges* and *Baies*. The use of opalescent glass, in which the glass is infused with a milky blue colour that refracts pink to yellow in certain natural and artificial light, has become synonymous with Lalique.

The technique was also used by several of his competitors, such as Sabino and Verlys in France and the British firm of Jobling, who retailed such wares under the (rather cheeky) tradename 'Opalique'. Examples charged with strong opalescence are particularly sought after. This effect is often dependent upon a pronounced variation in the thickness of a vessel and is seen to great effect in vases like *Bacchantes* and *Oran*. Another exceedingly rare type of grey glass used by Lalique is recognised today as 'Alexandrite' and has dichromatic properties, being capable of transmuting to near-pink when exposed to artificial light.

Above left:
Tourbillons. *A polished and black-enamelled vase, designed in 1926. This piece was available in other colours. Its Chinese-style bronze base was optional. Height 20 cm.*

Above right:
Oranges. *A satin-frosted and black-enamelled centrepiece vase, designed in 1926. Height 29 cm.*

Opposite:
Bacchantes. *Perhaps the most iconic of all Lalique's vases, this opalescent piece dates from 1927. It is seen here on an optional (and relatively rare) bronze stand. Height 24.5 cm.*

Above:
Ronces, *designed in 1921, was produced in several colours. This is the pale amber version. Height 24 cm.*

Above right:
Montmorency. *An opalescent vase, designed in 1930. Height 20 cm.*

When it came to subject matter, Lalique called upon his extensive knowledge of the natural world and the human form, along with a willingness to embrace and explore the possibilities offered by geometric forms. This was, after all, an age increasingly dominated by the skyscraper architecture and cubism-influenced style recognised today as Art Deco.

Full-scale production of vases appears to have begun in about 1913 and includes several varieties that enjoyed popularity well into the 1930s, including *Gui* (Mistletoe), *Monnaie du Pape* (Honesty Seeds) and *Ronces* (Briars). This last type was available in an extensive range of colours.

The period between the two world wars saw Lalique unleash a dazzling array of vases, each and every one of which demonstrated his talent for crafting bold and delicate motifs with innovative shapes. His acute understanding of botany is evident in vases such as *Mimosa*, *Acacia* and *Sauge*, whereas his *Violettes* vase in opalescent glass offers the perfect marriage of form and design by taking a band of slender-stemmed violet leaves and relief moulding them onto a wide and flared rim above a tapering body. His ability to formalise natural leaf formations into stylised repeated motifs works well with vases such as *Moissac* and *Malines*.

A masterly touch can also be seen in the *Languedoc* vase, whose clever combination of opaque green-coloured glass and a stylised design of tightly packed succulent leaves manages to evoke a sense of realism. Although a *Languedoc* vase is very desirable, many of the smaller foliate examples, featuring cheaper clear and frosted glass, are more readily available. Such vases were often embellished with colour staining to give additional emphasis to the leaf-inspired ornament. Flowers and fruit offered further inspiration and represented a significant percentage of Lalique's overall catalogue of inter-war productions.

On a grand scale, the aforementioned *Oran* vase, moulded in high relief with large chrysanthemum-type flower heads, uses both surface-polished and internal opalescence to optimum effect. The same techniques were employed to achieve similar results in berry-and-fruit offerings such as *Prunes* and *Montmorency*, alongside colour-stained backgrounds that help to accentuate the near three-dimensional modelling. *Rampillon* proved to be one of Lalique's most admired vases. It was moulded in relief, with three bands of pronounced diamond-shaped cabochons set against carpet reserves of millefiori. Although produced in several colours, as well as clear-and-frosted glass, this is yet another vase that benefits from opalescence, which lends it a dazzling jewel-like sparkle.

In tandem with his knowledge and appreciation of the botanical world, Lalique sought and found further inspiration from the wider animal kingdom, with birds, reptiles, amphibians, fish and insects providing a seemingly endless source of subject matter. His fondness for small birds such as sparrows and wrens is intimated in such

Oran. *A large thick-walled vase, designed in 1927. It shows the full potential of opalescent glass. Height 26 cm.*

Above: St François.
An opalescent and satin-frosted vase, designed in 1930, which illustrates Lalique's fondness for small birds. It proved extremely popular. Height 17.5 cm.

Above right: Coqs et Plumes. *A frosted and blue-stained vase, designed in 1928. Height 15.5 cm.*

vases as *St François* and *Petrarque*, albeit only in the loop handles of the latter. The same holds true for his cockerel designs, as might be expected from a staunchly patriotic Frenchman. The national bird of France takes a central role in his *Coq et Raisins* and *Coqs et Plumes* vases. The more exotic species were invariably designated to larger-scale vases that were also offered in several colour versions. His *Borromee* vase is mostly found in a deep cobalt blue and is decorated with numerous peacock heads shown in low relief above a swollen body and narrow foot rim. White peacocks are known to inhabit the Isola Madre, one of the three Borromean islands located in Italy's Lake Maggiore. One is thus left to assume that Ceylon (Ceylan – present-day Sri Lanka) is home to countless budgerigars and that the rivers of Formosa (Formose) are awash with long-tailed goldfish. Of these designs, *Ceylan* is perhaps his most endearing, being moulded with pairs of budgerigars on a cylindrical form that tapers towards its base. A flock of similar birds was used to good effect on larger-shouldered vases, where they appear perched among dense foliage, but on this occasion under the all-embracing title of *Perruches*. Once again, this particular piece was singled out for production in a wide range of translucent colours, being frosted and often enhanced with a thin white stain.

Lalique's *Aigrettes* vase saw him working in a distinctly Japanese manner, with several egrets defined by a blue-grey stain on a satin-frosted ground, depicted in flight beneath a wide top rim, their long tails more akin to those seen on a bird of paradise. *Tourterelles* makes use of an unadorned satin-frosted form tapering to a narrow neck supporting a cover sculpted with a pair of billing doves. The cover was eventually adapted and produced as a *presse-papier* (paperweight), but in both designs collectors might find it prudent to carefully examine the meeting point of the two birds' beaks, as this is an area where internal fractures have been found on some examples.

Fish have always suggested endless design possibilities to potters and glassmakers alike. However, in the hands of René Lalique, fish of all descriptions were depicted with great vibrancy, often conveying a sense of suspended animation. Lalique's fish appear on vases of many different sizes. *Formose*, at 17 cm, became one of his best-selling designs when it first appeared in 1929. The near-spherical form sits on a narrow circular foot rim and sports a short collar neck. The body itself is moulded in low relief, with numerous ornamental goldfish adorned with impressive and fronded tails.

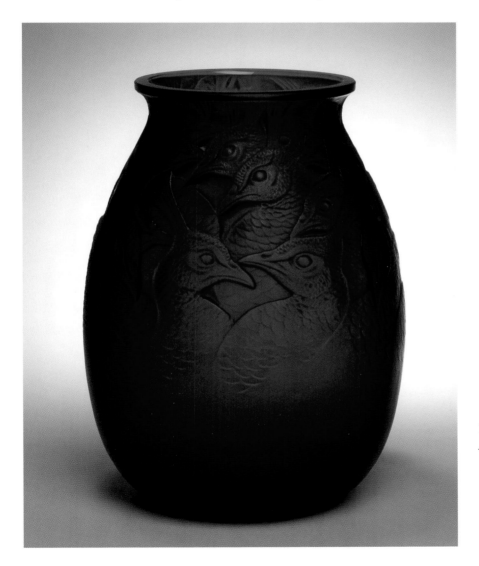

Borromee. *A satin-frosted and cobalt-blue vase, designed in 1928. Isola Madre is one of the three Borromean islands within Italy's Lake Maggiore and is populated by white peacocks. Height 23 cm.*

Above left:
Perruches. *An emerald green and dark-stained vase, designed in 1919. A popular vase produced in several colours. Height 26 cm.*

Above right:
Tourterelles. *A satin-frosted and opalescent vase and cover, designed in 1925. Height 28 cm.*

Left:
Margaret. *A thick-walled vase in topaz (a rare colour for Lalique), designed in 1929. The decoration of small birds in foliage is restricted to the angular handles. Height 29.5 cm.*

In contrast, *Oleron*, measuring a modest 9 cm, is quite literally smothered with a dense shoal of relatively mundane small fish and yet was considered worthy to be produced in opalescent glass when released onto the market in 1926.

At the other end of the spectrum, the *Poissons* vase measures a relatively modest 24.5 cm and depicts several overlapping large fish with spiked dorsal fins and pronounced heads of debatable beauty.

It might well have been its striking appearance that saw *Poissons* achieve popularity and become yet another candidate singled out for release in several colours. In stark contrast, *Penthièvre* is certainly the most geometric fish design to appear in the Lalique catalogue. Composed of several concentric bands of angel fish, the overall repeat effect is almost hypnotic. This radical design has been attributed by some authorities to Lalique's daughter Suzanne, who enjoyed a successful career working as a freelance designer for various French ceramic makers. In light of *Penthièvre*, the *Piriac* vase might be considered to represent a compromise

Poissons. *A cherry-red and satin-frosted vase designed in 1921. Height 24.5 cm.*

Penthièvre. *A dark amber and white-stained vase, designed in 1928. It is one of Lalique's most dynamic Art Deco pieces. Height 26 cm.*

by incorporating a pronounced band of naturalistic fish above a frieze of concentric and stylised waves shown in low relief.

Although insect subjects often appear to dominate Lalique's early jewellery creations, they seem to have played a lesser role when it came to his glass-design catalogue. Two notable exceptions among his vases are his *Sauterelles* (Grasshoppers) and *Gros Scarabees* (Scarab Beetles), both of large size and introduced in the early 1920s. *Gros Scarabees*, measuring 30 cm, would have offered a specific appeal to a western market already mesmerised by Egyptologist Howard Carter's discovery of the tomb of Tutankhamun and its fabulous treasure in 1922. Animal subjects on vases are also comparatively few, although they include several gazelle designs, a squirrel vase (*Senart*) and another showing a band of running hares (*Lièvres*). The horse appears on *Chevaux*, a cylindrical vase flared at the rim and moulded on the lower body with a frieze of several classical Greek-inspired horses set against towering vegetation. *Camargue*, by comparison, is a much bolder composition, featuring four shaped medallions of rearing steeds accentuated by colour staining and integral with a heavy and thickly walled vessel tapering towards the base.

Right:
Escargot. *A cherry-red and satin-frosted vase, designed in 1920, which shows Lalique's acute understanding of nature. Cherry red is one of the rarer colour options. Height 22 cm.*

Below left:
Camargue. *A satin-frosted and grey-stained vase, designed in 1942 but produced from 1947. This thick-walled piece was inspired by the famous horses found in the Camargue region of France. It was one of Lalique's last creations, remained unproduced until after his death in 1945. Height 29.5 cm.*

Below right:
Chevaux. *A satin-frosted and blue-stained opalescent vase, designed in 1930. Height 18.8 cm.*

Right: Danaides. *A satin-frosted and opalescent vase designed in 1926. This stylish and desirable vase was inspired by classical Greek sculpture. The top rim should be gently curved; a flat polished rim suggests the removal of a rim chip. Height 18.5 cm.*

Below: Terpsichore. *An opalescent vase, designed in 1937, whose theatrical subject makes this one of the most desirable examples in the Lalique catalogue. Height 20 cm.*

Nanking. *A clear and black-enamelled vase, designed in 1925 and considered the most Art Deco of all Lalique's vases. Height 34 cm.*

Reptiles appear to have met with a favourable response and for sheer drama *Serpent* is in a league of its own, representing the ultimate in commercial sculptural glass design. The coiled form of this powerful, huge-bodied snake can only hint at the potential hidden menace; yet it manages to present itself as a classic case where form dictates function, although its use as a vase might be seen as an unnecessary secondary consideration. (Its modern reproduction can be seen on page 114.) Lizards were the subject of a tapering bottle vase as early as 1908 and enjoyed further popularity when, in 1922, Lalique introduced his *Lezards et Bluets*, with a composition of opposing lizards interspaced by open cornflowers, all set upon a tapering vase with the same tapering collar neck. This is also one of very few vases offered for sale in polished and stained jet-black glass.

Figural subjects probably represent the most sought after and, by their very nature, the most seductive of all Lalique's design genre, with such vases still able to attract universal demand. The most celebrated is his *Bacchantes* vase, introduced in 1927

Above: Meandres. *A clear, frosted and stained vase, designed in 1934. Height 16.5 cm.*

Right: Marisa. *A grey, satin-frosted vase designed in 1927. Height: 24 cm.*

Below: Farandole. *A satin- frosted and blue-stained vase, designed in 1930. Height 17.5 cm.*

and sculpted in high relief with pairs of full-length naked maidens in poses evocative of both open revelry and suggestive intoxication. This blatant sensuality is seemingly enhanced when produced in a highly charged opalescent glass. Sadly, the fragility of so many heads and limbs modelled in such high relief means that many of these pieces have suffered damage over the years.

Lalique had adopted a more sober and statuesque depiction of the female form the previous year when he introduced his *Danaides* vase. Cast in low relief with a frieze of full-length naked maidens representing the daughters of Danas, each supports a large jar upon her right shoulder from which stylised torrents of water cascade to the feet. Once again, the more desirable vases feature opalescent glass and period staining, while special attention should be given to the top rims that should display a gentle 'roll over' feature (a flat polished top rim indicates the removal of later damage). Other vases such as *Bouchardon* and *Ronsard* are of simple form, being enhanced by the application of moulded and pierced figural handles to their shoulders. Both feature classical nude maidens holding or, as in the case of *Ronsard*, encircled by, floral swags. The overall effect in both instances is that of quiet elegance suggestive that less sometimes might offer more.

In a creative mind, where voluptuous bacchantes jostle for attention among enticing sirens (*sirènes*) and mysterious mermaids (*ondines*), alongside other gossamer-draped nymphs, the naked male might be considered an almost redundant source of inspiration. One of the few that appear to have enjoyed any commercial success is the vase entitled *Archers*. The subject matter shows several muscular archers aiming their bows and arrows skywards toward a convocation of menacing eagles. Introduced in 1922 in a shouldered ovoid form measuring 26 cm, this piece was produced in a wide range of colours. Another exception is *Palastre*, introduced in 1928, which is not only rare but also the second-tallest vase in Lalique's repertoire, standing at a monumental 40.5 cm. Composed of frosted glass, the tapering shouldered form is relief moulded with a frieze of naked Olympian athletes shown in varying poses, each enhanced by a thin sepia stain.

Soustons. *A frosted and sepia-stained vase designed in 1935. This design shows Lalique transposing a natural form into the prevailing Moderne style. Height 23 cm.*

With the arrival of the 1930s, the more traditional interpretation of Art Deco began to fade in preference to what at the time was seen as an equally radical, yet alternative, style recognised as Moderne. This more simplistic approach to design was rooted in the ideology promoted by such eminent early twentieth-century design schools as the Wiener Werkstätte in Austria and the Bauhaus School in Germany. Lalique might appear to have pre-empted this change in taste as early as 1925 with his *Nanking* vase, which makes use of decorative, geometric elements in a multi-faceted composition. Though less dramatic, the *Meandres* vase (1935) might be considered a more elegant design in tune with the artistic climate of that time. Here, Lalique uses a swollen cylindrical form tapering to the base and covers it with numerous polished serpentine bands against a textured surface that simulates acid cutting.

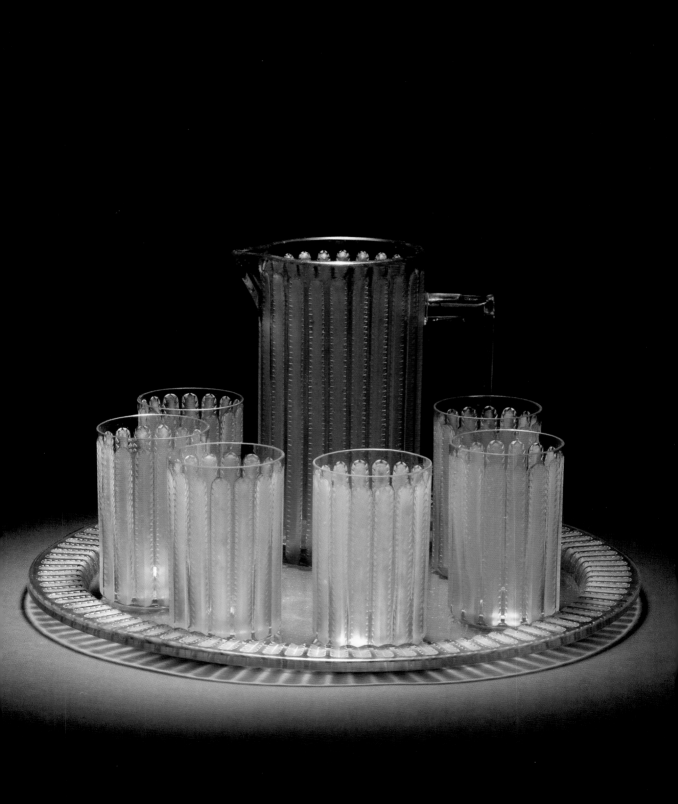

Chapter Four

BOXES, BOWLS, DISHES, TABLEWARE AND SMALLER OBJECTS

URING HIS EARLIER CAREER as a goldsmith and jeweller, René Lalique produced several small boxes in precious materials. In doing so, he was feeding a demand that could be traced back to the Middle Ages.

Although a number of these early works were inset with polished windows of clear rock crystal, boxes and caskets fashioned with glass panels in metal mounts only began to appear in quantity during the nineteenth century. Lalique, however, saw no reason for this and set about introducing a broad range of boxes and covers composed entirely from glass. They were soon to come second only to his vases in individual design and production numbers. Nearly all were destined for the lady's boudoir and were fashioned to receive face powders, pomades and other cosmetics; others were designed to hold cigarettes and jewellery. The most luxuriant and, as one might expect, the most expensive jewellery boxes were of rectangular panel form, fashioned from decorative exotic woods. The hinged covers and large key escutcheons were inset with foil-back glass panels moulded in low relief, with a choice of subject that included butterflies, chrysanthemums and stems of honesty flower seed-pods.

The forms and inspired subjects provided yet another stage upon which Lalique could perform. He introduced inventive and exciting boxes that demonstrated his virtuosity and skill to transform a utilitarian and potentially mundane object into a desirable work of art. Most of the boxes were circular, although at least two of his designs are known to be oval; others can be found in square, rectangular and even hexagonal section.

The decorative detail is usually surface moulded, with the notable exception of Lalique's large circular powder boxes, where great effect was achieved by relief moulding the design to the underside of the cover, leaving the top surface smooth and polished.

This technique produces an almost magical effect when used with opalescent glass, as in the *Deux Sirènes* mermaid box and cover. Lalique's choice of figural covers further demonstrated his sculptural abilities. Many appear to have enjoyed a lasting regard and include *Amour Assis*, with its cherub seated on a drum cover; and *Degas,* delicately modelled with an elegant ballerina-type maiden attired in an all-embracing gossamer gown that extends to a cylindrical base. Both subjects are surface frosted and further defined with colour staining. *Sultane* is applied in full relief: a sultry female nude figure shown seated, her legs are folded beneath her, her back is arched and her head gazes to the heavens. The square-section base is banded

Opposite
Jaffa. *An amber lemonade set, designed in 1931. The jug is 23 cm in height.*

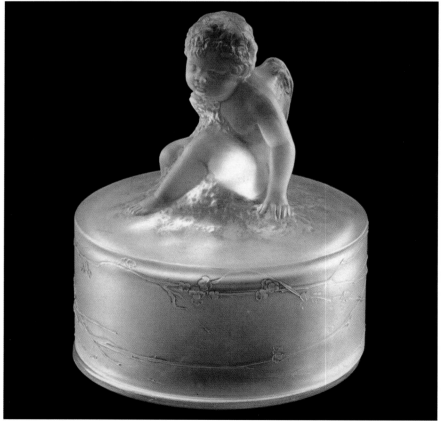

Above:
Figurines. *A frosted and sepia-stained panelled burr-wood box (or coffret), designed in 1914. Height 12 cm.*

Right:
Amour Assis. *A frosted and blue-stained box and figural cover, designed in 1919. Height 11.8 cm.*

in low relief, with an Art Deco stylised frieze. It is of a size suitable to accommodate cigarettes – presumably of Turkish origin, as intimated by the title.

Lalique managed to apply his ever-growing design catalogue to good effect by developing the range of boxes. Once again, figural subjects – including mermaids and nymphs – tend to be foremost in attracting attention, while the *Cleones* large powder box and cover, often found in pale amber glass, features scarab beetles and reflects the Egyptian revival prompted by events in the Valley of the Kings and the discovery of the tomb of Tutankhamun in 1922. In contrast, Lalique's *Houppes* powder box sports an all-over design of powder puffs, enhanced by the use of opalescent glass. This design was eventually licensed to the Coty company and can be found in printed form on all manner of Coty products, especially its cardboard powder boxes.

The production of tableware proved to be extremely lucrative and was eventually to account for a significant percentage of all Lalique's output. Numerous suites of table glass might include several sizes of vessel to accommodate red, white and dessert wines poured from matching decanters, while liqueur decanters and lemonade jugs and their matching glasses were occasionally found with circular trays. Lalique's wineglasses are relatively thin-walled and consequently vulnerable, whereas his lemonade sets make use of a far thicker glass and are therefore more resilient (they are also found in clear and pale amber glass). The term 'tableware' is an all-encompassing label that embraces not only decanters, carafes, drinking glasses, plates and dessert bowls, but also such diverse objects as menu-card holders, knife-rests, table jardinières and fruit bowls. Lalique could supply all of these, often with perfectly coordinated designs.

Roger. A clear-and-frosted box and cover designed in 1926. Diameter 13.5 cm.

Above:
Strasbourg. *Designed in 1926, this table service was offered with glasses of six different sizes and a large serving jug.*

Below:
Saint-Hubert. *A frosted-glass table jardinière, designed in 1927. Length 48.5 cm.*

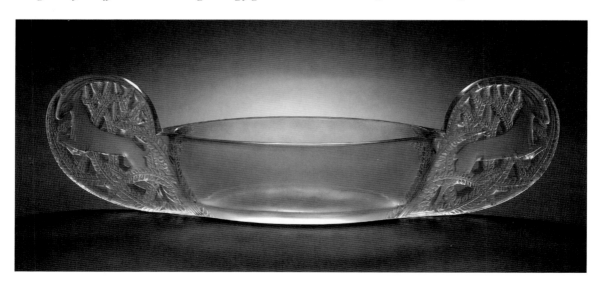

Above left:
Coquilles No.1.
*An opalescent plate,
designed in 1924.
This example is 30.3
cm in diameter, but five
sizes were available,
the smallest being*
Coquille No. 5
(diameter 17 cm).

Above: Prunelles.
*A clear, frosted and
sepia-stained claret jug
and stopper, designed in
1923. Height 25 cm.*

Left:
Deux Figurines.
*A pair of frosted and
stained menu-card
holders, introduced in
1924. Height 5 cm.*

One of the best-selling ranges was *Coquilles*, in which a clever composition of overlapping scallop shells was enhanced and defined with opalescence. Moulded on the underside, each plate, dish and bowl found support from each extremity. Lalique's table jardinières were created in a carefully chosen canoe form, with large ear-shaped handles intaglio moulded with floral motifs. His bowls and dishes offered a simple design canvas that he was able to both explore and exploit to great effect, with both established and new design categories that included several exciting animal subjects such as elephants and monkeys (as in *Madagascar*). Both are considered exceptionally rare, with monkeys featuring as an exterior band of twelve individual and highly pronounced monkey heads (presumably of a species native to Madagascar). Not only is this bowl found in frosted and opalescent glass, but also in a slightly deeper form with a gently domed base fitted at the rim with suspension hooks for use as a ceiling light. Sadly, some bowls of this type are known to have been cannibalised, with the individual monkey heads being adapted into pendants and brooches and then fitted into gilt metal mounts bearing spurious 'Lalique' marks.

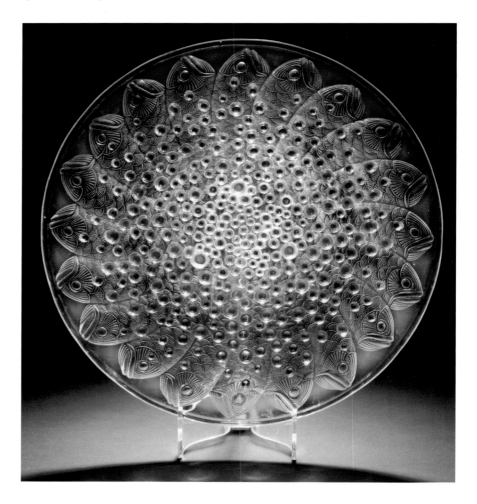

Roscoff. An opalescent dish with radiating fish, designed in 1932. Diameter 35 cm.

Chrysanthèmes.
An electric-blue and
white-stained circular
box designed in 1911.

Other design windows drew similar inspiration from the natural world, incorporating flowers, grasses and fish, with bowls and dishes such as *Lys* and *Volubilis* incorporating a more sculptural appeal with their accentuated stems adapted as supports. The theme of mistletoe was revisited in *Gui*, in which the pagan plant and its berries appear moulded on the exterior of the bowl (the berries playing the supporting role). More formalised flower heads are used on *Nemours*, a thickly walled bowl with bands of flowers deeply recessed, but heightened by colour stains and centred with black enamel. This bowl remains in production today, but in the full lead crystal with black enamel centres, devoid of staining.

A similar, but more naturalistic, treatment was given to a lily of the valley bowl, produced in both clear and opalescent glass and, on rare occasions, combined with peppermint green. With the onset of the 1930s, Lalique is recognised as having introduced a far more simplistic approach to some of his work. This can be seen in many of his wheatear and leaf designs. Another well-regarded design produced in an extensive range of plates, dishes and bowls made use of spiralling slender fish (*Poissons*) and was sold in both clear and opalescent versions. A more adventurous approach might be recognised in the *Anvers* and *Martigues* large bowl designs. The former makes play of a wide rim banded by fish, ensnared by bladderwrack seaweed; the latter shows a relatively formalised display of arched and whiskered fish encircling its outer rim.

Surprisingly few bird subjects found their way onto bowls, but one design in particular proved to be very popular. *Perruches* made use of a frieze of budgerigars

Above: Perruches. *An opalescent bowl designed in 1931, which was also produced in clear glass and a rare peppermint green (shown on back cover). Diameter 24.5 cm.*

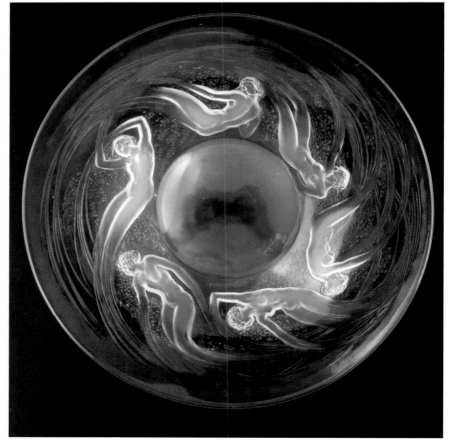

Right: Ondines. *An opalescent bowl, designed in 1921. This is the* ouverte *model, which measures 21 cm in diameter and shows an upright top rim; the alternative version (*refermée*) has a gentle fold-over top rim and is slightly smaller, at 19 cm.*

set against dense foliage and was produced in both clear and opalescent glass, as well as a particularly rare version that also blended opalescence with a peppermint-green colour (see back cover illustration).

As with most of Lalique's subject material, maximum appeal is once again offered by his opalescent figural offerings, especially in his bowls and plates, such as the *Ondines* design, which features numerous mermaids in a turbulent sea. The theme was later reworked as *Calypso*, with a more stylised Art Deco treatment and to great effect on a large charger. Mermaids or sirens also appeared either solo, as with *Trepied Sirène* (a large table charger raised upon three short feet), or in pairs, as seen in *Sirènes*.

The *1932 Catalogue des Verrieres de René Lalique*, which is available in a reprinted format, goes some way to illustrating the sheer variety coming from the company's Wingen-sur-Moder glass factory. It is impossible to cover each and every category in detail here, but what might be considered some of Lalique's more obscure objects are invariably of gifted form and eagerly sought by enthusiasts. The catalogue illustrates that, for Lalique, glass desk furniture included not only inkwells and blotters, but also seals, bookends and ashtrays. In all, no fewer than fourteen inkwells (*encriers*) feature in the catalogue. These, as might be expected, encompass much of his design repertoire. However, one of the earliest inkwells features an owl design worked in black glass, an example of which is presently on display in the Glass gallery of the Victoria and Albert Museum in London.

Lalique's catalogue shows an equally impressive black-glass inkwell of panelled box form, decorated with deer heightened with a pale grey wash. Despite being introduced as early as 1910, the subject matter appears to pre-empt classic Art Deco

Biches. *A black-glass inkwell, cover and stand, designed in 1913 and measuring 15 cm square.*

Faune et Nymphe.
*A rare example of a rocker blotter (*buvard*), designed in 1920 and featuring frosted glass.*
Length 16 cm.

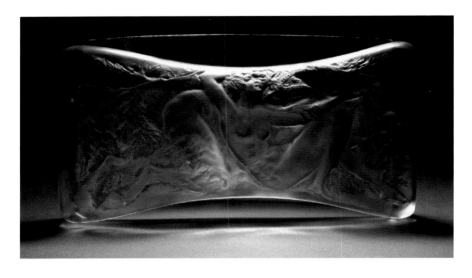

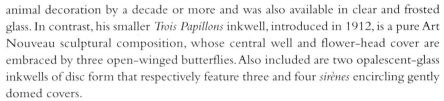

animal decoration by a decade or more and was also available in clear and frosted glass. In contrast, his smaller *Trois Papillons* inkwell, introduced in 1912, is a pure Art Nouveau sculptural composition, whose central well and flower-head cover are embraced by three open-winged butterflies. Also included are two opalescent-glass inkwells of disc form that respectively feature three and four *sirènes* encircling gently domed covers.

Deux Figurines.
A hand mirror with integral white-metal back plate, designed in 1913.
Length 35.3 cm.

Rocker blotters (*buvards*) are relatively rare. They tend to be moulded with motifs that include flora and fruit; others feature pairs of seated mermaids, as well as a nymph with her attendant faun. Seals (*cachets*) are equally rare, but cover a wide range of animal and bird subjects and were available plain, although one could have one's initials incise cut at additional cost. In comparison, ashtrays (*cendriers*) appear to be more plentiful and are found in clear, frosted, opalescent and occasionally coloured glass as well as in circular, oval, square and rectangular section. Subject matter includes pairs of wood nymphs (*Medicis*), male athletes (*Archers*), as well as several flower heads and others of Art Deco heavy geometric form.

Most of Lalique's hand mirror designs belong to his earliest production period and feature Art Nouveau maidens, butterflies, flora, dragonflies and the figure of Narcissus. *Narcisse Couchée* is thought to have been initially designed in about 1908 and the reclining classical subject is modelled in low relief, gazing at his own reflection. He is confined within a shaped panel at the juncture of the circular mirror and slender tapering handle. This picture of vanity leads us to assume that Lalique's intention was to offer a

Muguet et Hirondelles.
*A frosted photo frame,
designed in 1939.
Height 39.5 cm.*

humorous, if gentle, reminder to the user to avoid excessive use. Others quite literally mirrored in construction the circular polished-bronze mirrors associated with the Orient and made use of piercing to receive a colourful silk tassel or an applied, slender hand grip of elliptical outline. Subject matter was limited to four compositions, featuring lily of the valley, peacocks, rearing goats and a pair of secretary-type birds. Wall mirrors were occasionally an optional addition to the bottles and cosmetic jars and covers that constituted his extensive range of 'Garniture de Toilette'. Lalique's *Epines* (Thorns) and *Eglantines* (Wild Roses) mirrors were composed of six sectional panels moulded with relevant decoration around circular foil-backed mirrors measuring an impressive 43 cm in diameter and, at 2,800 francs, were priced higher than virtually all the vases in the 1932 catalogue.

Lalique also offered a selection of easel-backed picture frames, some being of square section, others rectangular. These could feature in any part of the home. His choice of thematic detail included cornflowers, lilies, flocks of swallows, birds perched among berry-laden branches and an example moulded with myriad graduated star motifs.

Chapter Five

CAR MASCOTS AND PAPERWEIGHTS

Lalique is known to have produced individual designs for a range of thirty car mascots, with twenty-nine making it into production by 1932. Car mascots are probably the most highly contested of all his statuettes, being pursued by Lalique enthusiasts and car enthusiasts alike.

Car mascots (known as hood ornaments in the USA) became popular in the 1920s. They usually take the form of a shape or figure that symbolises the car manufacturer. Initially being a way of decorating a car's radiator cap, they became works of art in their own right. Perhaps the most famous example is the *Spirit of Ecstasy* figure, which first appeared on Rolls-Royce models in 1911.

Paperweights, on the other hand, had been introduced in about 1910 and among many designs may be found *Tourterelles*, modelled as two billing turtle doves, and two opposing eagle heads contesting a large cabochon pearl between their open beaks while set upon a shallow rectangular base. Many of the paperweight models that followed made use of panel-form polished plinths of rectangular section, with the three-dimensional subjects frosted in contrast.

On such paperweights can be found cats, owls, deer, antelope, moose, bison, bulls, rhinoceroses and an elephant. Several intended car mascots were also adapted as paperweights, while others were similarly modified as bookends, being fitted onto polished mounts in black glass or veined marble. These include the eagle's head (*Tête d'Aigle*), horse's head (*Longchamp*) and standing cockerel (*Coq Houdan*) designs. It has been suggested that the eagle's-head mascots were destined for the staff cars of the German military. As a staunchly patriotic Frenchman, it seems unlikely that Lalique would have ever considered accepting such a commission. It should also be remembered that the factory in Wingen-sur-Moder was in an area that was occupied by German forces early in the Second World War. The entire region had been contested and claimed by both nations for several centuries and had only recently been ceded to France as part of the reparations inflicted on Germany after the Treaty of Versailles in 1919.

The Breves Galleries, located in London's fashionable Knightsbridge, had become the premier retailer for Lalique glass and a company newspaper advertisement dating back to the early 1930s announced that car mascots were available at 2 guineas (or 3 guineas if mounted on one's car bonnet). Such mounts incorporated a dynamo-powered light bulb and were able to secure both the mascot itself and an internal coloured glass disc of red, green, blue, mauve, amber or white. The Breves literature waxes lyrical, stating: 'The motor mascots designed by Lalique achieve a rare combination of beauty and distinction. They are made from a special glass, untarnishable and almost unbreakable. At night their charm is enhanced by

Opposite:
Victoire. *Perhaps the most iconic of all Lalique's car mascots, this exotic piece is satin frosted and polished. It was designed in 1928. Length 25.6 cm.*

Comete. *A clear-and-polished car mascot, shown fitted in its original Breves Galleries mount. Height 19 cm. (Courtesy of Christie's.)*

concealed illumination in soft colours'. However, in practice neither claim could be substantiated, thanks to stone damage and the effect of prolonged sunlight, whose ultraviolet rays caused some clear-glass mascots to transmute to a pale amethyst colour. Consequently, many were only able to display their full dramatic appeal after dark, although legislation in the United Kingdom eventually banned their illumination, as the additional frontal lighting was considered a distraction to drivers.

The first Lalique mascot was commissioned in 1925 by Citroën and was cleverly modelled as five leaping horses in profile. *Cinq Chevaux* (Five Horses) was specifically designed for the car of the same name and horsepower. The *Comete* car mascot appeared soon after and, as with the examples that followed, was not designed for any particular car and as such was a 'Maison Lalique' creation. Sculpted as a highly stylised and faceted five-point star, an inferred sense of speed is reinforced by its integral flared tail.

Deux Aigles. *A frosted-and-polished paperweight, designed in 1914. Length 10 cm.*

The subjects that followed over a period of little more than five years demonstrated the versatility both of Lalique's imagination and his sculptural perception. The designs appear to have been introduced in no thematic order. All were available in frosted-and-polished clear glass, although several were produced in an optional opalescent or semi-translucent coloured glass, which adds to their appeal and value. The designs include several birds, such as a swallow with raised wings and tail feathers (*Hirondelle*), a falcon (*Faucon*), a standing cockerel (*Coq Houdan*), a cockerel with raised tail feathers (*Coq Nain*), a cockerel's head (*Tête de Coq*), an eagle's head (*Tête d'Aigle*), a peacock's head (*Tête de Paon*), a hawk's head (*Tête d'Epervier*) and an owl (*Hibou*, the rarest of these bird subjects).

Cinq Chevaux. *This was Lalique's first car mascot, being commissioned by the Citroën Motor Company in 1925. Height 15 cm.*

Above:
Faucon. *A clear-and-polished car mascot, designed in 1925. Height 15 cm.*

Above right:
Grande Libellule.
A frosted-and-polished mascot, designed in 1928. Height 21 cm.

Right:
Tête de Belier. *A satin-frosted car mascot, designed in 1928. Height 9 cm.*

The animals include a ram's head (*Tête de Belier*), while *Epsom* and *Longchamp* feature two powerfully sculpted heads of racehorses, as their titles suggest. *Longchamp* is known to have been made in two different versions, one having a double mane. The rarest animal mascot is the fox (*Renard*), which was modelled in angular fashion, standing on all fours with alert expression and voluminous tail. It is also considered to be the rarest of all Lalique's car mascots. The only fish subject is a perch (*Perche*), sculpted with erect dorsal fins and which has an aquatic friend in the shape of a seated frog (*Grenouille*).

The insect world is represented by two stylised dragonflies. The smaller, *Petite Libellule*, has retracted wings, while the larger (*Grande Libellule*) is modelled with wings aloft. Disc-shaped mascots incorporate intaglio-moulded and frosted subjects that include St Christopher (*St Christophe*) and a kneeling male nude archer (*Archer*). A similar, but near-elliptical, panel-form mascot was used to incorporate a greyhound (*Lévrier*) running at speed.

Figural mascots include: *Chrysis*, a female nude modelled kneeling with her back arched and her arms behind her head; *Sirène*, featuring a seated mermaid clutching a shell to one ear, and *Vitesse*, which depicts a female nude thrusting forward in a pose that asserts her position as an emblem of speed. Perhaps the most dramatic of all Lalique's figural mascots is *Victoire* (Spirit of the Wind), which features the head of an open-mouthed Amazon. The sense of theatre is heightened by her stylised windswept hair, the length of which to the tip of her nose is of extreme importance, as many have been ground shorter to remove chip damage (see page 78).

Above left:
Vitesse. *A satin-frosted opalescent car mascot, designed in 1929. Height 18.5 cm.*

Above:
Coq Nain. *A frosted-and-polished mascot, designed 1928. Height 20.5 cm.*

Chapter 6

CLOCKS, SCULPTURE AND *CIRE PERDUE*

A S CLOCKS AND TIMEPIECES often provided a focal point in many rooms during this period, Lalique was not alone in recognising that they should also be an eye-catching work of art in their own right – not only fit for purpose, but also a positive enhancement to any interior.

Strictly speaking, a timepiece simply displays the time, whereas a clock has the additional feature of a striking mechanism to chime the hours and (usually) the quarter-hours. This book will refer to all as 'clocks', although the majority were actually timepieces. Of course, the actual mechanisms tend to be of almost secondary importance, as enthusiasts are usually more concerned with the condition of the glass surrounds.

In Lalique's 1932 catalogue, these items are divided, dependent on size and mechanism, into 'Pendules' and 'Pendulettes'. The larger examples are invariably of substantial thickness and can exceed 3 cm, with their chosen decorative motifs intaglio moulded into the reverse and accentuated with acid frosting. The most dynamic and celebrated of Lalique's larger clocks is *Le Jour et la Nuit* (Day and Night). This exquisite piece features male (day) and female (night) nude figures, whose sensual forms are entwined around a disc surround and an electric mechanism. Lalique manages to suggest the opposing times of day by relief moulding the female figure and intaglio moulding her male partner, thereby achieving contrasting densities of darkness and light. Each clock was supported on a bronze, tapered panel plinth, fitted with an internal light bulb which, when illuminated, provided an ambient light that accentuated the nude couple and the clock face. This particular model was retailed in several colours, including dazzling electric blue, grey and an exceptionally rare topaz colour, where the brown-hued body transmutes to deep amethyst in the denser female figure.

In contrast, the *Deux Figurines* clock is of arched-panel outline, moulded with a relatively sedate composition of two graceful classical maidens shown garnishing the central electric clock face with a floral wreath. Once again, the thick glass panel is supported on an illuminated bronze plinth, which makes great play of the maidens' diaphanous gowns, whose folds partially reveal their elegant, yet blatantly sensual, forms.

Lalique's smaller clocks appear to have been designed to grace either a mantelpiece, or a bedside or dressing table. The mantelpiece clocks are usually of square- or arched-panel form and can be found moulded in low relief with floral or bird designs. They were produced in clear, frosted, stained and opalescent glass. Others, such as the *Roitelets* design, are of circular panel form and stand 20 cm high. They are encircled by a flock of stylised wrens, whose outer wings lend a 'sawtooth' appearance to the surround.

Opposite:
Le Jour et la Nuit.
This electric clock in electric blue is supported on a bronze stand fitted for illumination. It was designed in 1926 and, at a height of 37.4 cm, is one of Lalique's larger examples.

Deux Figurines.
*A clear-and-frosted electric
clock, designed in 1926,
that illustrates Lalique's
versatility as a designer,
working with a
romanticised neo-classical
theme, while achieving
a perfectly balanced
composition.
Height 38 cm.*

Naiades. *A clear-and-
frosted eight-day clock,
designed in 1926.
Height 11.3 cm.*

Most of these clocks appear to have been fitted with ATO electrical mechanisms and dials, purchasers being given the option of a decorative or a relatively plain face. The bedside and 'toilette' clocks are prime examples of Lalique's desire to give the same careful and considered approach to what might be considered the most simplistic of panel forms. The finished results are little short of magical, and nowhere is this more apparent than in the *Naiades* clock, whose square-section glass surround is enveloped by six nubile long-haired water nymphs, who jostle around the clockwork mechanism and plain dial. Although usually more desirable when found in opalescent glass, this is one design that actually appears to benefit from the more simple clear-and-frosted technique, as it offers a stronger definition of the complex design.

The most popular pattern appears to be *Inséperables*, which features two pairs of budgerigars perched upon flowering branches as they flank the central dial. Fitted

Deux Colombes.
A frosted and blue-stained electric clock, designed in 1926. Height 22.2 cm.

Above:
Deux Coqs. *A satin-frosted and clear clock, designed in 1939.*

Left:
Quatre Moineaux du Japon *in pale amber, designed in 1928. Height 18.5 cm.*

Opposite left:
Source de la Fontaine: Doris. *A frosted statuette on a wooden base, designed in 1924. Height of figure 63 cm.*

Opposite right:
Grande Nue (bras leves). *A satin-frosted statuette, designed in 1921. Height of figure 52 cm.*

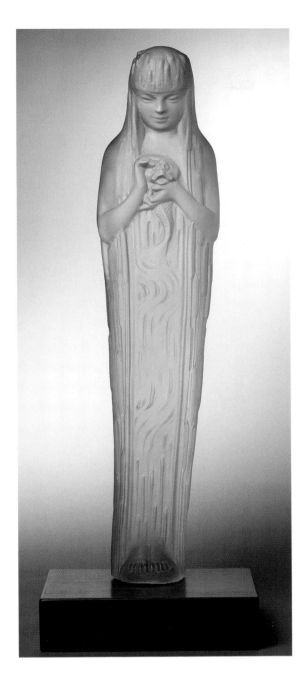

with the same mechanism this design was also produced in clear and opalescent glass. Many customers chose a relatively plain clock face, but other options featured small birds among branches. Customers could also select a protective, leather travelling case, although few of these appear to have survived.

Lalique's earliest interest in bronze sculpture prompted him, at the age of twenty, to enrol for lessons at the École Bernard Palissy in Paris. It was here that he nurtured an

Detail from Source de la Fontaine: Doris.

obvious aptitude, which he was then able to develop in his works of art and early glass creations. In later years, he was to marry Augustine-Alice Ledru, the daughter of the celebrated French sculptor and contemporary of Rodin, Auguste Ledru, thereby acquiring a wife and a potential technical advisor and critic.

Lalique's attention concentrated primarily on relatively small-scale sculptures that focused on the female form in various ways. Others may manage to capture the grace identifiable with the classical age of the ancient Greeks, whose womenfolk were often attired in diaphanous drapery that readily accentuated their hidden slender forms. But Lalique's sculptural prowess and fascination with the female form allowed him to push the boundaries of his imagination and explore the optical possibilities presented by the glass itself. The *Source de la Fontaine* statuettes that adorned his 50-metre fountain at the Paris Exposition of 1925 accounted not only for some of his tallest figures, but also his most extensive range, numbering at least fourteen known individually named figures modelled in seven different heights. Each was sculpted as a slender tapering water maiden, adorned with an integral headdress and gown while holding an individual attribute at her chest. The range varied in height from 43 cm at the top to 70 cm at the base.

Three of these figures were illustrated in the 1932 catalogue, but thirteen variants are actually listed as being available at prices ranging from 1,350 francs up to 1,900 francs, depending on size. Those shown in the catalogue are mounted on mahogany plinths. Other large figures include the *Grande Nue (bras leves)*, which – at 66 cm – is his next-largest individual sculpture and features a naked maiden standing with legs together and both arms raised in a pose suggesting supplication. Once again, the statuette is mounted on a wooden plinth and fitted for electric illumination. It cost 1,750 francs. At the other end of the scale, Lalique's smallest sculptures are his seals (*cachets*), destined for both gentlemen's and ladies' writing desks. The *Statuette Drapée* measured 6.5 cm, while others, such as his bas relief *Victoire*, a mere 4.5 cm. It is, however, the mid-size figures that appear to have been the most popular, especially his statuettes of *Suzanne* and the slightly rarer *Thais*. Both feature a nubile maiden with arms outstretched in support of floor-length gossamer drapery with head

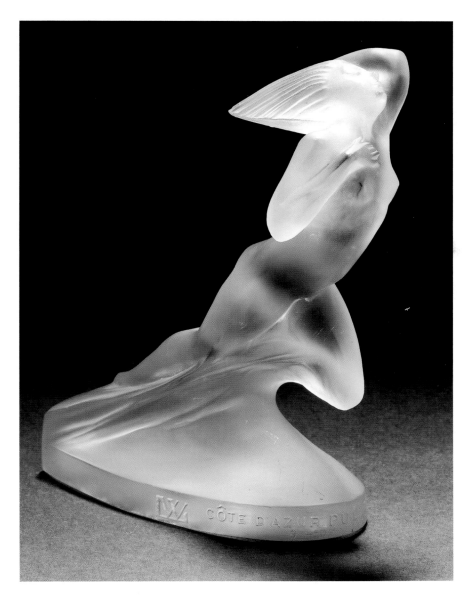

Côte d'Azur.
A satin-frosted statuette commissioned by the Compagnie Internationale des Wagons-Lits and distributed to commemorate the inauguration of its luxury train service to Vintimille and the Côte d'Azur.

inclined to the shoulder and with one knee raised. Both measure 23 cm high. The only obvious difference is that the figure of *Suzanne* (see front cover) features pierced drapery in the upper arms, although her head is inclined to her right and her knee to her left in direct opposition to that of *Thaïs*.

Other figures that found lasting favour include *Sirènes*, depicting a twin-finned mermaid shown seated while holding a shell to her ear. Being 10 cm high, it was also adapted as a car mascot. The same applied to the similar, but larger, figure titled *Naiade*, which – at 13 cm – is also the rarer of the two.

In 1929, Lalique was commissioned to provide a commemorative statuette for the inauguration of the Côte d'Azur Pullman Express, along with decorative glass

Six Cigales. *A Cire Perdue frosted-and-stained glass vase, created 1919. The shoulders are modelled and covered with open-winged Cicadas. Height 8 cm. (Courtesy Mr Andrew Stewart)*

panels for the railway carriage interiors. Produced in frosted glass, the dynamic figure was modelled as a maiden with stylised windswept hair, lunging forwards from an integral base lettered in low relief and with the insignia of the Compagnie Internationale des Wagons-Lits.

Lalique's initial efforts to exploit the sculptural potential offered by glass began during the later years of his initial career as goldsmith and jeweller. These early pieces were mostly produced using a technique that dated back to antiquity, known as *cire perdue* (or the 'lost wax' process). This involves modelling the desired vase or figure in wax and then supporting and encasing it within a wooden box, into which is then poured a semi-liquid refractory clay in which the wax model or 'maquette' is immersed. The clay is then allowed to set hard and a small hole is bored into both the top and bottom of the solid mould. The mould is then heated, allowing the melted wax to escape through the lower drilled aperture, which is eventually sealed with clay. The interior of the mould now houses the original detail that had been modelled onto the wax maquette and is ready to receive the molten glass, which in the case of a solid figure, is simply poured into the void or, if a vase, blown into the same and then left to slowly cool in order that the glass is properly annealed. In order to retrieve the now-encased glass, it is necessary to carefully break the mould, thereby making any such glass *cire perdue* object totally unique. Once exposed, the item is then carefully trimmed or receives further detail before being subjected to surface polishing, frosting or staining.

Once complete, the Lalique factory would use a wheel to cut an 'R. Lalique' or 'Lalique' signature into the piece. This might also include two sets of numbers: the first is thought to be a reference number; the second is the last two digits of the relevant year of manufacture.

Cire perdue vases and figures represent the most desirable of Lalique's glass creations and, although no complete illustrated records exist, the actual number of items produced using this technique is thought to number a tiny percentage of his total output, in contrast to the many thousands created out of reusable steel moulds.

The question as to whether such pieces might have been modelled in wax by Lalique himself has been debated for many years by scholars and enthusiasts. In certain instances, the hand modelling of the original wax maquette has retained incredibly detailed surface fingerprints which, had Monsieur Lalique ever fallen foul of the law and had his fingerprints taken, might have offered an open-and-shut case. Alas, René Jules Lalique proved to be a model citizen and the debate continues.

The subject matter found in this small number of figures and vases reflect the rest of his catalogue inventory: however, the very nature of these lost-wax pieces often allowed for the sort of pronounced detail and undercutting that was impossible to

A cire perdue *vase of ovoid form, modelled with pairs of budgerigars among blossoming branches in high and low relief, heightened with green staining, c. 1914. Height 25 cm. (Courtesy of the Gulbenkian Museum, Lisbon.)*

A cire perdue *vase. The upper body is cast in low relief, with a frieze of mice among foliage heightened with grey staining. Signed 'R. Lalique', the piece dates from 1913. Height 18.5 cm. (Courtesy of the Gulbenkian Museum, Lisbon.)*

Feuilles Fougères. *A* cire perdue *vase, created on 11 February 1929, modelled at the shoulders with a pair of unfurling ferns heightened with grey staining. Height 12.5 cm. This vase was discovered by the author while taking part in a BBC 'Antiques Roadshow' held at Dumfries House in Scotland in 2008. The owner had purchased it complete with a plant for £1 at a car boot sale a few years earlier. It was sold at auction that same year for £26,000 plus buyer's premium.*

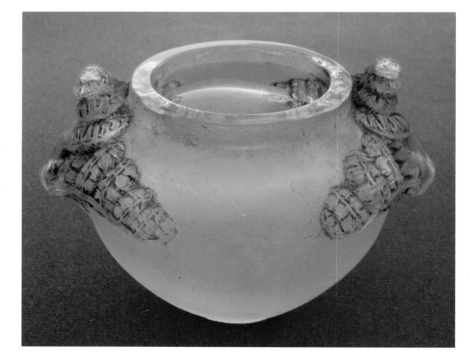

emulate with standard moulds. A vase in the Gulbenkian Museum in Lisbon shows this to great effect. Dating from 1914, it features pairs of budgerigars perched upon gnarled branches of flowering *prunus* with their bodies in high relief and heads in total relief.

Lalique was to return to the same topical matter in various vases, bowls and clocks throughout his career as a glass designer and maker. His interest in this method of creating such unique pieces had begun during his earlier career as a jeweller, but continued well into his later life.

Suzanne. *An opalescent statuette, shown here on an optional bronze plinth of tapered-panel type, fitted for illumination to give an ambient light.*

Chapter Seven

ARCHITECTURE AND LIGHTING

WHEN RENÉ LALIQUE walked into his new Parisian home at No. 40 Cours la Reine in 1904, he was entering a property built to his own exacting standards. It was – and still is – a five-storey testament to his remarkable imagination and intimate appreciation of the natural world.

The house was built in collaboration with an architect called Feine, although the foundation stone bears the name 'R Lalique' and nothing more. The exterior is carved in white stone, with carefully positioned pine trees that feign structural support and flank the massive entrance. Their branches reach across and into the large cast-iron doors, allowing the continuous decorative detail to merge across the grid of individual semi-translucent glass panels. The façade is adorned with organic ornament and suggests a house which has evolved naturally.

Lalique had been experimenting with glass reliefs at the small glassworks on his family estate in Clairefontaine. That venture appears to have lasted for little more than a decade, but the Cours la Reine house is without question a structure in which Lalique allowed his sculptural fantasies to be expressed on a truly grand scale. The result of this expression is one of the most important buildings of the twentieth century, whose beauty begs the question: why, having created such a landmark, was Lalique not inundated with commissions for similar residences?

The exterior of this architectural treasure still exists, although the street has since been renamed Cours Albert Premier. It may be found on the north bank of the River Seine, close to the Pont de Inca, with a view that looks over the river to the Eiffel Tower. Though still standing proud, it is tucked away in a row of relatively non-descript buildings, with not a single tourist in sight. The interior has been given over to offices, but perhaps one day someone will rescue it and return it to its original splendour as a lasting memorial to the shy designer who was to live and work there until his death in 1945.

Although Lalique does not appear to have been involved in designing other complete buildings, he did find himself commissioned to design several architectural interiors after the First World War. One notable exception appears to be the 1913 commission from François Coty to design and manufacture windows for his New York gallery at 712 Fifth Avenue. The floral-decorated windows are known to have been made at the Clairefontaine glassworks and still survive *in situ* in uptown Manhattan.

In 1922, Lalique was asked to offer a design for a dining room at the Pavillon de Marsan of the Musée des Arts Décoratifs for the Exposition des Arts Decorateurs. Here, he provided a central chandelier and numerous glass partitions, echoing the theme of his own residence with frosted foliage. It was, however, his contribution

Above: No. 40 Cours la Reine (now Cours Albert Premier), the residence of René Lalique from 1904 until his death in 1945.

Above right: Carved detail above the glass panel door.

Right: Window balcony, featuring carved detail and wrought-iron pine cone railing. (Courtesy of Oliver Knowles.)

to the 1925 Paris Éxposition des Arts Décoratifs et Industriels Modernes that was to elevate his international reputation as a master interior and exterior architectural designer even higher. The event was attended by twenty-one nations, Germany conspicuous by its absence, although it was essentially a showcase for French luxury goods. Lalique's contribution was evident not only in his own pavilion but also in those of the 'Sevres Porcelain' and 'Parfumerie Français'. His personal pavilion had been designed in collaboration with the architect Marc Ducluzand and housed a display that concentrated on his unique *cire perdue* creations arranged in cabinets that encircled a massive 6-foot glass vase composed of glass panels detailed with rearing horses and acanthus foliage.

Above:
Ceylan. *An opalescent
vase adapted as a table
lamp base with associated
celluloid shade hand-
painted with budgerigar
decoration. The vase was
designed in 1924.
Height of vase 24 cm.*

Above right:
*René Lalique at the time
of the 1925 Paris
Exposition, seen
examining a Charmes
frosted-glass ceiling bowl.*

Right:
*Lalique's frosted-glass
panels in situ on one of
the railway carriages of the
Compagnie Internationale
des Wagons-Lit.
(Courtesy of Lalique.)*

Detail of the glass panels Lalique designed in 1928 for the Côte d'Azur service of the Compagnie Internationale des Wagons-Lits. The panels lent much to the overall opulence of the train's interior. (Courtesy of Lalique.)

Lalique's external architectural work dominated the Esplanade des Invalides and, at 50 metres in height, towered over the surrounding pavilions. This was his illuminated fountain, comprising seventeen graduated tiers, each supporting eight slender glass statuettes of water nymphs in fourteen individual variations of attire. After the closure of the event and the dismantling of the structure, Lalique continued to offer these *Source de la Fontaine* figures for sale in his catalogue, mounted on mahogany box plinths. He designed several other fountains, including one the following year for the nearby Arcades des Champs-Elysées, for which he provided the local interior and street lighting. While in London, he also provided a fountain for the Daily Mail Ideal Home Exhibition of 1931. None, however, were ever on such a colossal scale as that seen at the 1925 Paris Exposition.

In 1926, Lalique turned his attention to the internal and external architectural decoration for the Cannes showrooms of the House of Worth and created a striking Moderne entrance with illuminated frosted-glass surrounds and shop sign set against a façade of black marble. He was also commissioned later in 1929 to provide decorative glass panels for the Pullman rail carriages on the Compagnie Internationale des Wagons-Lits' Côte d'Azur train. These feature male and female nudes against fruiting vines, reminiscent of his *Bacchantes* vase. Rectangular panels modelled with numerous classical Olympians were also produced as over-door plaques for the entrance foyer of Claridge's Hotel in London and still survive *in situ* while their 122 cm length represents an unrecognised technical achievement of that age. Probably his most recognised and fêted interior is that installed in St Matthew's Church at Millbrook on the Channel Island of Jersey.

Always referred to as the 'Glass Church', from the exterior it seems anything but; yet the entrance doors inset with a pair of near life-size satin-frosted glass angels can only hint at the breathtaking interior that awaits the visitor. Commissioned in 1934 by Florence, Lady Trent, it was conceived as a fitting memorial to her late husband Jesse Boot, First Baron Trent of Nottingham, who had amassed a fortune through his nationwide chain of chemist shops. The church itself had been built during the Victorian period and was now subject to a total renovation instigated by Lady Trent, who knew Lalique personally as a neighbour when staying at her villa in the south of France.

Lalique provided a high altar before a free-standing illuminated cross frosted and moulded with stem-and-leaf decoration, flanked by side pillars similarly moulded, but surmounted by lush lilies. The 'Madonna' and 'Jersey Lily' floral motifs are also repeated in the glass screens, which separate the side chapels from the Lady Chapel. They include a reredos of four illuminated angels, similar to those that greet visitors at the entrance. Lalique also included a glass font, which rests on a narrow pedestal base composed of crimped panels, and whose wide cylindrical basin is frosted with a geometric frieze. The ceiling itself is fitted with recessed strip lighting behind frosted-glass panels which, along with the screen and altar illumination, offer an ambient light that engenders an atmosphere of peace and tranquillity within a space that also celebrates modernity. Unfortunately, Lalique's other great interior is long gone.

The SS *Normandie* made her maiden voyage in 1935 and has long been regarded as a veritable floating temple to, and ultimate expression of, the finest in French Art Deco design. Lalique's contribution was to be found in the impressive 91-metre first-class dining room. Guests were greeted at the entrance by a massive chandelier before they made their way to their respective tables between twelve monumental tiered and illuminated glass structures that bordered and towered over them. In 1942, the vessel was requisitioned by the US government while harboured in New York and was undergoing conversion into a troopship before a much-debated on-board fire resulted in total devastation. The ship capsized and was eventually scrapped. It is, however, lighting on a more human scale for which Lalique is best remembered and his restless imagination conjured up a fascinating catalogue of inventive light fixtures. Into this category might be included his 'Surtout Décoratifs',

Left: The 'Glass Church': St Matthew's, Millbrook on the Channel Island of Jersey.

Below: The nave and altar of St Matthew's Church. The Lalique free-standing cross was moulded with stem-and-leaf decoration.

although the light source was primarily placed to illuminate the panel or sculpture, being usually hidden within in a bronze plinth or panel base. Panels were usually of rectangular section but might also be shaped or semi-circular, as can be seen in his dramatic *Oiseau de Feu* (Firebird), which measures 43 cm high.

The thick glass panel of the *Oiseau de Feu* is intaglio moulded and frosted, the wings of the mythical bird being outstretched from the torso of an exotically plumed maiden. Other panels showed small birds gathered among bare branches, while the more adventurous feature *Trois Paons* (Three Peacocks) or *Deux Cavaliers* depicting knights engaged in mortal combat on rearing warhorses. Also within this category are two large fish sculptures that appear in Lalique's 1932 catalogue under the individual titles of *Gros Poisson Algue*s and *Gros Poisson Vague*s. Both are often found mounted in bronze tapering plinths incise cast with stylised seaweed. The thick and consequently heavy forms were produced in clear and polished glass.

Other lighting devices retailed under the all-encompassing title '*motifs décoratif*' include a series of individual lights whose general appearance is similar to Lalique's more adventurous perfume bottles. Produced on a grander scale, these *Tiara Veuilleuse* were designed as ambient light sculptures destined for tables or architectural niches. The shouldered, bottle-shape base is fitted with an internal light; a large crescent panel that descends just short of the base is then fitted into the narrow neck. The bases are often vertically ribbed and frosted and raised on bronze plinths. The decoration was intaglio moulded into the reverse and then frosted with

The first-class dining room of the SS Normandie, c. 1935, featuring Lalique's coffered ceiling and massive light features.

Opposite: Lalique's magnificent angel screen at St Matthew's Church.

Right: Rameaux.
A frosted and sienna-stained table candlestick designed at around the same time as the maiden voyage of the SS Normandie in 1935. Height 20 cm.

Opposite:
Lausanne. *A satin-frosted and opalescent ceiling light with original suspension cords, designed in 1929. Diameter: 38 cm.*

designs that included peacocks, cupids, apple blossom, dandelions and Japanese hawthorn. They were made in two sizes: the larger ones measure 40 cm; the smaller examples, at 18 cm, were destined for the dressing table or bedside and feature almond blossom, rose and carnation ornamentation.

Lalique also offered an extensive selection of lighting, including table lamps, chandeliers, wall lights, candlesticks and ceiling bowls. The bowls were more affordable and therefore more popular; as a result, they tend to be easier to find. The choice of motifs included the usual floral, fruit and figural subjects, with the figures proving most popular, especially Lalique's mermaid-like *Sirènes*, produced in opalescent glass. Animal subjects also appear in a variation on a bowl featuring a frieze of twelve monkey or lemur heads modelled in high relief and retailed under the name *Madagascar*. The ceiling light has the subtle difference of being slightly taller and gently domed on the underside; it is also pierced around the top rim and fitted with hooks to receive silk cords. Probably the most frequently found ceiling bowls are the *Coquilles*, which are usually in opalescent glass and which, in

Dahlias. *A frosted ceiling light, designed 1921. Diameter 30 cm.*

Charmes. *A ceiling light with four clear, frosted rectangular support panels, designed in 1924. Diameter 34 cm.*

Belier. A clear, frosted and sienna-stained lamp de cheminée with pleated-silk shade, designed 1931. It was available with two alternative narrow glass shades. Height 30.5 cm.

most cases, were intended as table bowls before being converted. Such conversions were made by drilling the rims and inserting hooks or rings to receive silk suspension cords.

This type of hemispherical bowl is known to have been cut into two sections and adapted as wall lights by the Breves Galleries, Lalique's premier London retailer in Knightsbridge. The company even adapted vases such as *Ceylan* and *Formose* as lamp bases and offered the option of a celluloid shade with a matching hand-painted design. The Knightsbridge firm is said to have made these 'alterations' with Lalique's

Paons. *A satin-frosted and grey-stained table lamp, designed in 1910. Height 42.5 cm.*

Bague Personnages.
A satin-frosted and grey-stained table lamp, designed in 1913. Height 44.5 cm. (Inset) detail of the interchangeable collar (bague) with figural moulded decoration.

agreement, but this writer is not totally convinced. They also provided their own mounts to receive and illuminate Lalique's range of car mascots.

Lalique's clear understanding of the refractive properties of glass was of fundamental importance when he turned his attention to lighting and the effects that he sought to achieve. Consequently the passage of light through an intaglio-moulded and frosted panel or a relatively simple ceiling bowl was a key consideration that influenced his intended design.

One of Lalique's first table lamps was on the drawing board as early as 1910 and featured that favoured bird of many an Art Nouveau artist and craftsman: the peacock. The tapered panelled stem of the lamp enclosed four birds, with their exotic tail feathers pendant to the square base. The gently domed cover included a symmetrical version of the birds in full display, the decoration being heightened with sepia or grey staining. The *Cardamine* table lamp introduced in 1928, however, is pure Moderne with its upright panel support intaglio moulded with a formalised stem-and-tendril motif supporting a satin-frosted and fluted box shade. Another variation came in the form of a table up-lighter, whose tapering and incise-moulded stem and spreading circular base supported an inverted and flared shade of similar section. Made in satin-frosted clear glass, this particular model was

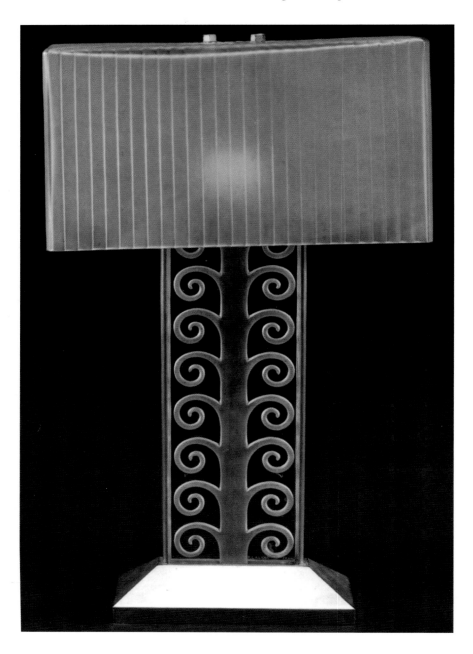

Cardamine. *This clear-and-frosted table lamp and shade show Lalique's talent for the Moderne style. It was designed in 1928. Height 40.8 cm.*

Grande Boule de Gui.
*A frosted and panel-form
ceiling light, designed in
1922. Diameter 50 cm.
(Courtesy of Christie's.)*

available with a choice of three decorative collars (*bagues*) moulded with serpent, figural or foliage detail.

Lalique's pendant light fittings (*lustres*) were inventive and sometimes included a central bowl and radiating segments that offered a stellar effect; his larger and heavier examples once again represented a more Moderne approach. These *lustres* make use of thick intaglio-moulded and frosted panels that radiate around a stainless-steel mount in the manner of a monumental lemon squeezer. Decorative themes include birds, berries and leaves, and geometric motifs, with some examples incorporating light shades and others with totally enclosed illumination that produces a soft diffused lighting. Others, such as the *Grande Boule de Gui*, were constructed as a spectacular large ball composed of several individual segments moulded with an overall mistletoe theme. The segments were connected by metal rings and the clear-and-frosted glass was enhanced with a choice of coloured stains.

Chapter Eight

POST-WAR AND THE TWENTY-FIRST CENTURY

BY THE END OF THE 1940s, the Lalique company was concentrating all its efforts through the Wingen-sur-Moder glassworks, having closed the Combs-la-Ville factory in 1937. Sadly, René Lalique was never to see the result of the German withdrawal from his Wingen works, as he died in Paris on 5 May 1945, shortly before the unconditional surrender by Germany to the Allies.

It was down to René's son Marc to restore the factory site and revive the fortunes of the company in fragile post-war Europe. Being the son of René Lalique must have been a daunting responsibility at the best of times, let alone when the need to take the reins of the family business arose. According to those who had known him or made his acquaintance, Marc appears to have inherited the same reserved personality as his father; yet, since joining the family business in 1922, he had displayed strengths that helped to establish his own credentials and enabled him to make his all-important contribution in reasserting the company's position as the premier French glassmaker. Not least of these were his indisputable business acumen, and marketing and organisational skills on which his father had come to depend through the difficult years that followed the Wall Street Crash of 1929.

Marc Lalique soon showed his talent as a highly competent designer in his own right, with an eye on the post-war market and its demand for simpler abstract forms emanating from Italy and Scandinavia. More important was his ability to achieve change without compromising the long-established 'Lalique' ethos that demanded the combination of design excellence and exciting innovation. Probably Marc's most important decision was to make fundamental changes to the actual type of glass used by moving to a full lead crystal that incorporated 24 per cent by volume, or double the amount of lead oxide that had been used in the manufacture of demi-crystal. The implementation of the new mix appears to have occurred in about 1950 and had the immediate effect of producing a much whiter glass. The company continued to produce and occasionally modify pre-war designs; however when marked by acid stencil or engraved script the initial 'R' (for René) was removed. Later engraved script marks offer some confusion by the presence of an 'R' within a small circle after the name, but this is merely a registration symbol. It is also important to be aware that the designs produced in pre-war moulds still carried a moulded signature that retained the 'R'. However, they can be differentiated by the post-war use of the whiter full lead crystal body (or 'metal' when referring to glass), when compared to the distinctly grey glass of the inter-war years.

Opposite:
Serpent. *A red and satin frosted vase, designed in 1928 and reintroduced in 2010.*

The Lalique catalogue now concentrated on clear and frosted designs, avoiding coloured glass and staining. The use of opalescent glass was phased out in the 1950s. In 1951, Marc Lalique announced his intentions to the world at the Pavillon de Marsan 'Art of Glass' Exhibition, showing a highly personal and distinct debut collection that managed to avoid any visual inferences to his late father. Marc was making it clear that this was a new era with new ideas and a new guiding spirit made manifest as 'Cristal Lalique'. The new designs included exciting tableware, such as what came to be his most popular wineglass, *Ange*, designed in 1948 and said to be inspired by a carved angel in Reims Cathedral. The wineglass stands at 20.5 cm and

Above: Marc Lalique in his design studio, c. 1955.

Left: Ange. *A frosted and engraved champagne glass sometimes referred to as* The Angel of Reims. *It was designed by Marc Lalique c. 1947. Height 20.5 cm.*

Above: Ingrid. *A black and satin-frosted vase by Marc Lalique, c. 1960. Originally in clear and frosted glass, but revived in black, c. 2008. Height 26.5 cm.*

Below: A Bacchantes *vase prior to finishing and acid frosting.*

Above: Craftsmen at the Wingen glassworks filling a mould with a gather of molten glass attached to a steel pontil rod.

Below: Engraving the Lalique signature onto the base of a vase.

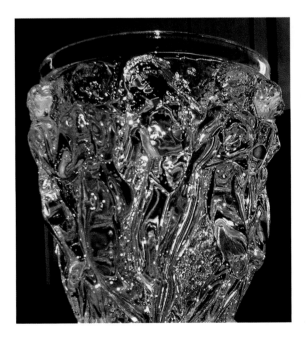

is moulded with the image of an angel, whose head and shoulders support the slender bowl enveloped by its engraved wings.

The 'Roxane' tableware issued in the 1960s takes a similar, but secular, approach by featuring naked maidens sculpted in an embrace. This motif was also adapted in a larger size as the matching decanter stopper and the central feature of an ashtray. However, the introduction of these new designs came at a comparatively slower

Marie-Claude Lalique, c. 1990, dressed in 1930s style. Her jacket is adorned with a pre-war glass brooch designed by her grandfather, René Lalique.

rate than the almost frenetic pace of design release instigated by René Lalique. They did, however, include innovative yet stylish lighting, complemented by elegant mirrors and the now-iconic *Cactus* table. The same accolade might similarly apply to Marc's remarkable table centrepiece, which features a pair of swans on a mirrored plateau cut with a rippled effect. Eagle-eyed readers of a certain age might well remember their regular appearance on the dining table of the Southfork Ranch in the American television show *Dallas* during the late 1970s and early '80s.

Contracts from the perfumer Nina Ricci helped to revive the company's perfume bottle manufacturing base by commissioning more than 50 per cent of its commercial output from Lalique. Together with Marc's daughter, Marie-Claude, the company was credited with introducing in excess of thirty-five new perfume bottles during this period, including nine 'Maison' designs for public sale.

Dragons. *A 'Maison Lalique' clear and gold-coloured vase, designed in 1996. Height 28 cm.*

Right: Zeila Noir.
A panther designed by
Marie-Claude Lalique,
c. *2000.*
Length 36.5 cm.

Below: L 'Air Du
Temps. *perfume bottle*
created by Robert Ricci
and designed by Marc
Lalique in 1947,
produced in four sizes.
This example 10.5 cm.

Two Nina Ricci bottles qualify as probably being the most recognisable of all Marc's designs: *L'Air du Temps* (1947), with its distinctive frosted doves-in-flight stopper; and *Coeur Joie* (1942), which took the form of an open heart. However, according to Glenn and Mary Lou Utt in their essential *Lalique Perfume Bottles* (1990), this bottle was 'from an original idea by Robert Ricci', son of Nina.

Other perfume bottles, such as *Requête* (designed for Worth in 1944) still managed to encapsulate the modernity of the machine age, suggestive in its cog-like composition and tapering stopper with flat top incise moulded with the letter 'W'. Expert opinion is divided as to whether this particular design is the work of the father or the son. The same modernity is evident in pre-war bottles, especially others commissioned by Worth for its *Je Reviens* and *Imprudence* essences. Marc Lalique was responsible for redesigning the respective stoppers for ease of removal. These post-war productions are signed 'Lalique' (without the 'R' prefix); the later *Je Reviens* bottles are fitted with pale blue plastic stoppers.

In addition to introducing new and inventive designs, Marc Lalique's lasting legacy was the expansion of the company's retail network in Europe and particularly in the USA, which became an important overseas market. In 1956, he was joined by his daughter Marie-Claude after she had completed her education at the École des Arts Décoratifs in Paris. It soon became obvious that her artistic philosophy shared a far greater synergy with the work of her father than that of her

grandfather. She was fortunate in having a studio not only at the Wingen works, but also at her grandfather's former magnificent home and atelier at No. 40 Cours Albert Premier in Paris.

When Marc Lalique died in 1977, Marie-Claude assumed the position of designer, although she avoided the dual role of Head Administrator previously held by her father. The company itself passed into the ownership of the French company Pochet, which was keen to emphasise the artistic control, direction and continuity being determined and implemented by René Lalique's granddaughter. Marie-Claude's willingness to experiment was evident in her range of figural sculptures and vases. Her 1970s 'Singing Colours' selection, for example, showed her readiness to reintroduce the use of contrasting coloured glass. Her untimely death in 2003

Antinea. A clear and ocean blue vase designed by Marie-Claude Lalique, c. 1980 and reintroduced in 2010. Height 20 cm.

Right: Nu Assis. *Black and satin-frosted seated nudes, designed by Marie-Claude Lalique, c. 2000.*

Below: Silvio Denz, the owner and Chairman of Lalique and a devoted collector.

Below right: Aurora. A 'Maison Lalique' clear-and-frosted vase, designed in 2008. Height 30 cm.

robbed the company of an inspired free spirit which had so much more to give. Future generations might be better placed properly to assess both Marie-Claude's and Marc Lalique's artistic input and importance to the company. Any future retrospective of their work will hopefully enable their individual contributions to emerge from beyond the shadow of the presently all-prevailing phenomena that was, and remains, René Lalique.

Today, the company is owned by Art & Fragrance, which was founded in 2000 and is based in Zollikerberg near Zurich. It also owns the Daum glassworks in Nancy and the prestigious Haviland porcelain manufacturer of Limoges. It is cheering to note that the company chairman, Silvio Denz, is a devotee of all things Lalique.

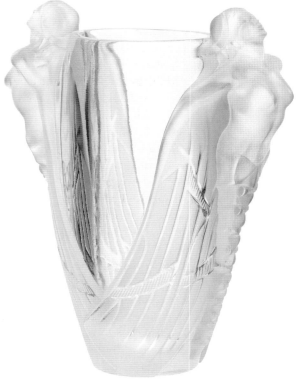

LALIQUE TIMELINE

1860 René Jules Lalique born on 6 April in Ay, Marne, France.

1862 Lalique family moves to Paris.

1872 Attends Lycée Turgot and wins a design award.

1876 Father dies; René gains an apprenticeship with the Parisian jeweller, Louis Aucoc.

1878 Moves to London to attend the Sydenham School of Art.

1880 Returns to Paris and begins work as a freelance designer for relation called Vuileret, working on textiles and wallpaper. Studies sculpture under Justin Lequien at the École Bernard Palissy.

1881 Works as a jewellery illustrator for Auguste Petit fils on the Rue de Chabanais.

1884 Concentrates on jewellery design, selling to several top jewellery houses with his friend Varenne acting in partnership as his agent. 'Lalique et Varenne' work from No. 84 Rue de Vaugirard in Paris.

1885 Purchases his own jewellery workshop from Jules Destape at Place Gaillon in Paris.

1886 Marries Marie-Louise Lambert.

1887 Leases a second atelier on the Rue du Quatre-Septembre.

1889 Vever and Boucheron include works by Lalique (anonymously) in their displays.

1890 Leases larger premises at No. 20 Rue Thérèse; moves into apartment on third floor of new premises. Now employs thirty craftsmen. Meets Augustine-Alice Ledru.

1891 Introduced to Sarah Bernhardt by his friend the artist Georges Clairin. Begins experiments with glass at No. 20 Rue Thérèse.

1892 Birth of his daughter, Suzanne, by Augustine-Alice Ledru.

1894 Designs stage jewels for Sarah Bernhardt.

1897 Awarded the Croix de la Legion d'Honneur.

1900 Receives international acclaim at the Exposition Universelle in Paris. Birth of his first son, Marc, by Augustine-Alice Ledru.

1902 Marries Augustine-Alice Ledru on 8 July. Sets up a small glassworks with a staff of four at the family estate in Clairefontaine, producing moulded plate glass.

1904 Travels to the United States and exhibits at the St Louis World's Fair. Moves into his new home at No. 40 Cours la Reine (now Cours Albert Premier) in Paris.

1905 Opens his first retail shop at No. 24 Place Vendôme in Paris.

1907 Approached by his neighbour François Coty to design embossed gilt paper label for bottles made by Baccarat. Lalique agrees but only if given the responsibility of designing the glass perfume bottles. Same bottles then made by Legras et Cie in Paris. Acquires larger glassworks at Combs-la-Ville, near Fontainebleau. Death of his second wife, Augustine-Alice née Ledru.

A cire perdue *bronze*
figure of René Lalique,
sculpted by Theodore
Louis-Auguste Riviere,
c. *1900–04.*
(Courtesy of Glenn
and Mary Lou Utt.)

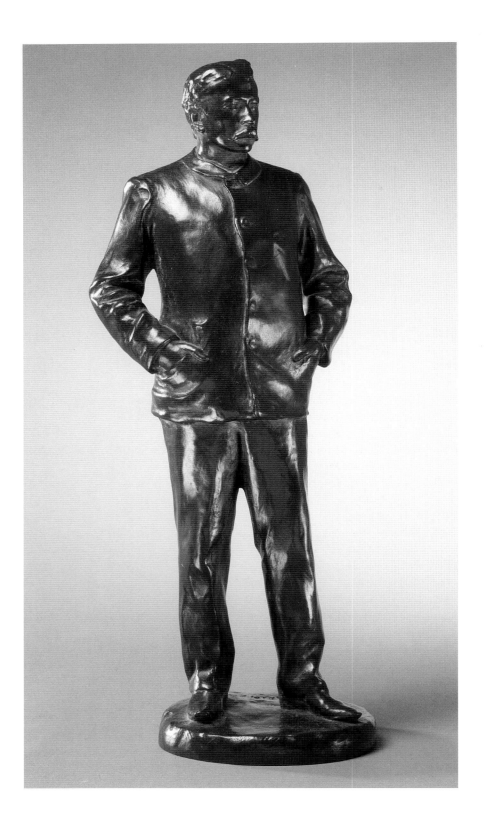

1909 Combs-la-Ville glassworks becomes fully operational, with a staff of between fifty and one hundred.

1910 Death of his first daughter, Georgette, by his first marriage to Marie-Louise née Lambert.

1911 First glass exhibition at the Place Vendôme showrooms.

1913 Provides decorative glass windows for Coty's New York showrooms at 712 Fifth Avenue (now Henri Bendel's store).

1914 Closes Combs-la-Ville glassworks upon the outbreak of the First World War.

1918 Reopens Combs-la-Ville glassworks.

1921 Opens larger glassworks at Wingen-sur-Moder, near Strasbourg.

1921 Achieves considerable acclaim providing glass fittings for the luxury liner *Paris*.

1925 Achieves further acclaim at the 1925 Exposition Internationale des Arts Décoratifs et Industriels Modernes in Paris. Commissioned by Citroën to produce his first car mascot *Cinq Chevaux*. Birth of his second son, Jean Raymond, by Marie Anre on 30 March.

1927 Provides architectural glass surround for Worth's Cannes showrooms.

1927 Achieves acclaim providing glass fittings for the luxury liner *Ile de France*. Birth Renée Jeanne Georgette, by Marie Anre.

1929 Commissioned to provide figural glass panels for Compagnie Internationale des Wagons-Lit Côte d'Azur Pullman Express railway carriages.

1930 Breves Galleries, London, publish the catalogue *Lalique Lights and Decorations*. Designs main doors for Prince Asaka Yasuhiko's palace in Tokyo, Japan.

1932 Publishes *Catalogue des Verrieres de René Lalique*.

1933 Retrospective exhibition of Lalique's work shown at the Musée des Arts Décoratifs in Paris.

1934 Commissioned to provide glass interior for St Matthew's Church, Millbrook, Jersey, in collaboration with the British architect A. B. Grayson.

1935 Achieves further acclaim for providing glass fittings in the first-class dining room on the luxury liner *Normandie*. Opens new showrooms in the Rue Royale which continue to operate as the company's premier showrooms.

1937 The Combs-la-Ville glassworks is closed.

1939–45 The Wingen glassworks is closed during the German occupation.

1945 Lalique dies in Paris on 5 May; Marc Lalique takes over the company.

1951 Marc Lalique introduces his new range of full lead crystal glassware at the Pavillon de Marsan 'Art of Glass' Exhibition.

1956 Marc Lalique's daughter, Marie-Claude, joins the company.

1977 Marc Lalique dies. Marie-Claude remains as company art director but the company is sold to Pochet.

2003 Marie-Claude Lalique dies at the age of 67.

2008 The company is purchased by Art & Fragrance under the chairmanship of businessman and Lalique collector Silvio Denz.

BIBLIOGRAPHY

Arwas, Victor. *Lalique Glass*. New York, 1980.

Barten, Sigrid. *René Lalique Schmuck und Objects d' art 1890–1910*. Munich, 1977.

Bayer, Patricia and Waller, Mark. *The Art of René Lalique*. London, 1988.

Becker, Vivienne. *The Jewellery of René Lalique*. London, 1987.

Brunhammer, Yvonne (editor). *The Jewels of Lalique*. Paris, 1998.

Dawes, Nicholas. *Lalique Glass*. New York and London, 1986.

Hatch, Carolyn. *Deco Lalique*. Royal Ontario Museum, Toronto, 2006.

Lalique, Marc and Marie-Claude. *Lalique par Lalique*. Paris, 1977.

Lefkowith, Christie Mayer. *The Art of René Lalique Flacons and Powder Boxes*. New York, 2010.

Leite, Maria Fernanda Passos. *René Lalique at the Calouste Gulbenkian Museum*. Lisbon, 2008.

Malevski, Mirek and Waller, Mark. 'Les Mascottes de Lalique', in *Automobiles Classique*, Summer 1985, pp.114–122.

Marcilhac, Felix. *R. Lalique, Catalogue Raisonne de L'Oeuvre De Verre*. Paris, 1989.

McClinton, Katherine Morrison. *Lalique for Collectors*. New York, 1975.

McDonald, Jesse. *Lalique*. London, 1995.

Mortimer, Tony L., *Lalique Jewellery and Glassware*. London, 1989.

Percy, Christopher Vane. *The Glass of Lalique*. New York and London, 1975.

Sherwood, Shirley, *Venice Simplon-Orient Express*. London, 1985.

Utt, Mary Lou and Glenn with Bayer, Patricia. *Lalique Perfume Bottles*. London, 1991.

Catalogue des Verrieres de René Lalique 1932. Limited-edition reprint for Japan Exhibition, organised by Kiya Gallery Tokyo and Gallery 25. London, 1982.

Poseïdon à Maison Lalique. *A clear blue vase designed in 2004. Height 29.5 cm.*

INDEX

Page numbers in italics refer to illustrations